D0971658

FATHERING

List of Contributors

Charlotte Holt Clinebell, Ph.D.
  Psychotherapist in private practice, Claremont, California
  Extension Professor, University of California, Riverside, California

Howard Clinebell, Ph.D.
  Professor of Pastoral Counseling, Southern California School of Theology, Claremont, California

Theodore A. Gill, Th.D.
  Provost and Professor of Philosophy, John Jay College of Criminal Justice, New York, New York

William A. Kelly, S.T.M.
  Psychotherapist in private practice, Carmel Valley, California

William M. Lamers, Jr., M.D.
  Assistant Clinical Professor of Psychiatry, University of California, San Francisco, California

John L. Maes, Ph.D.
  Director, Mountainview Associates, Psychotherapy and Human Relations Consultation, Rindge, New Hampshire

Edward V. Stein, Ph.D.
  Professor of Psychology, San Francisco Theological Seminary (San Anselmo) and Graduate Theological Union, Berkeley, California

Ann Belford Ulanov, Ph.D.
  Member of the Board of the C. G. Jung Institute for Analytical Psychology, New York, New York
  Psychotherapist in private practice
  Professor of Psychiatry and Religion, Union Theological Seminary, New York, New York

FATHERING
fact
or
fable?

Edited by

Edward V. Stein

ABINGDON / Nashville

BF
723
P25
F37

FATHERING: FACT OR FABLE?

Copyright © 1977 by Abingdon

Library of Congress Cataloging in Publication Data

Fathering, fact or fable?
   1. Father and child. 2. Child psychology.
I. Stein, Edward V.
BF723.P25F37   155.6'462   76-56840

ISBN 0-687-12864-1

Text on pages 11-29 originally appeared in *The Journal of Pastoral Care* (March, 1974) and appears with the permission of the editor.

Text on page 88 is from "A Memory of Youth" from *The Collected Poems of W. B. Yeats.* Copyright 1916 by Macmillan Publishing Co., Inc., renewed 1944 by Bertha Georgie Yeats. Reprinted by permission of The Macmillan Company.

Text on pages 91-92 is from "The Sad Shepherd" from *The Collected Poems of W. B. Yeats.* Copyright 1906 by Macmillan Publishing Co., Inc., renewed 1934 by William Butler Yeats. Reprinted by permission of The Macmillan Company.

Scripture quotations noted RSV are from the Revised Standard Version Common Bible, copyright © 1973.

Scripture quotations noted NEB are from The New English Bible. © the Delegates of the Oxford University Press and the Syndics of the Cambridge University Press 1961, 1970. Reprinted by permission.

MANUFACTURED BY THE PARTHENON PRESS AT
NASHVILLE, TENNESSEE, UNITED STATES OF AMERICA

Contents

To
John, Bob, Kay, and Helen,
who shared with me the same
caring father and mother.

Preface

This book began a million years ago when some hirsute male stood at the mouth of his cave, exhausted from an unsuccessful three-day caribou hunt and, listening to the wailing of hungry stomachs behind him, looked out on a lightning storm. He began to wonder what it would be like to be up there with all that power and how he would use it. With one bolt he would kill and roast enough meat to turn that racket behind him into burps and laughter for days.

Once his imagination got him skyborne, investing all that space with maxi-fathers, it was only a matter of time till night brought them back to earth, mixing it up with earth mothers who stayed in the cave and kept the fire. It is not hard to see how fathers were "out there" sky people and mothers were the ones who knew and guarded the dark, inner depths of the cave where life flickered and sometimes grew into a flame, sometimes went out.

Fantasy went wild. The storyteller went on peopling the sky with gods and god-ing the sky with people. They weren't always pleasant forms for the Greeks, but they were believably familial. As the Greeks told it, Mother Earth and Father Heaven (*Gaia* and *Ouranos*) gave birth to all sorts of half-human monsters and it was only after many universe-rattling wars and child-devouring intrigues that Zeus finally ended up with a planet ready for humans.

It is not hard to see that the Greek storytellers were men

7

because, as they told it, for a long time—the so-called Golden Age—the earth was inhabited only by men. Woman was created by Zeus in a moment of anger at Prometheus whose fire-stealing ambition irritated Zeus. Pandora (Edith Hamilton calls her a "beautiful disaster") was sent to earth as the first woman, with a box not exactly laden with goodies— Freudian symbolism for the womb's gift to history.

So for the Greeks and Romans, as for the Hebrews and Babylonians and many another series of storytellers, the world was embroiled in a family quarrel from the beginning involving tyrannical fathers, conniving mothers, and war- ring, patricidal sons and daughters. Power and fecundity seemed to be the focal problems. In our time, fecundity is taken for granted. Power is now the issue. Who gets it, who deserves it, how it is used, what it has to do with male and female, how it surrounds the infant in that crucible of the psyche, the family, and whether it is benign or malignant constitute the repetitive and current themes of the human drama.

Whether we human beings can consciously unravel the complexities, which for eons we have largely lived out unconsciously, is our burning question. As we move into an age of role debriefing and an undoing of the cave–sky imagery that has so long coded our doing and being as fathers and mothers, it seems important to ask what parenting really is.

This book deals with only half the problem: fathering. That is partly because, like most such events, it just *grew* rather than being conceived whole on paper.

While on sabbatical in Zürich three years ago, I was asked to speak at the University of Helsinki. I chose the topic "Fathering: Fact or Fable." The address was published the following year in the United States and appears as the introductory chapter. Sitting over coffee in a New Orleans café last year, a friend said he had read it and asked why I didn't do a book on it. My response was, "Great! How about helping me!" His contribution appears as chapter 6. I am also grateful to Bill Kelly for generous assistance in other ways.

The reader will soon see that fathering is one end of a polar reality. We do not pretend otherwise. We would like to have encompassed parenting, but it is felt that sharpening differences is as likely to heighten truth as a bland merging. We have included a feminine perspective in two chapters.

Although a variety of psychiatric, therapeutic, theological, and sociological refractions will be evident, with only one exception all the writers are parents. That should say something about the theory.

I dislike introductions that tell you what the writers are going to say. There are some pleasant surprises. There is some valuable help for parents, therapists, pastors, teachers, sociologists, students, and anyone concerned about the shifting human scene.

Here are new ways of looking at fathering, new sensitivities to its importance, a challenge to our old stereotypes, a refreshing theological foray, moving moments with a grieving father, practical words for those with absent fathers, fathers seeking guidance, children needing refathering, and next steps for those leaning into the future. The last two chapters by the husband-and-wife pair among our authors offer alternatives for tomorrow.

Two further chapters had been intended and contracted for this book: "The Black Father" and "The Father in Myth." The manuscript was held over several months in the hope that these could be included. Personal tragedies in each instance and printing deadlines unfortunately necessitated launching the work without the much desired completeness these would have added.

I wish to express here my deep thanks to the busy

professionals who gave so generously of their time to make this volume possible and to Thelma Furste and Loel Millar for their patient assembling and typing of the manuscript.

We also wish to thank the Editor for permission to use in its entirety the article "Fathering: Fact or Fable?" which first appeared in *The Journal of Pastoral Care* in March, 1974.

Edward V. Stein

Chapter 1

Fathering: Fact or Fable?

Edward V. Stein

There are at least two kinds of fathering: biological and psychological. Biological fathering is a brief, easy, and usually satisfying enterprise. Psychological fathering, on the other hand, may take the better part of a lifetime, is very difficult to do well, and has peaks and valleys of anguish that would try a god.

Biological fathering is a task in the world's surplus population that, except for its more immediate physical gratification, has shifted from a central objective to a peripheral one. Through artificial means, a few well-chosen males could supply enough sperm to repopulate the whole earth. Whether the egos of the men would survive the inflation (or their bodies the malice) that such recognition would provoke is conjectural.

Psychological fathering, however, is what the world is in need of more than ever in its history. There is a considerable body of scholarly evidence that civilization will stand or fall with whether such fathering is available in sufficient quantity.

The impact of psychological fathering first hit me with full power when I was working with suicidally depressed patients in San Francisco General Hospital a few years ago. I was co-therapist in a group that met each Monday evening in the psychiatric ward, and most of them had attempted suicide at one time or another. They ranged in age from late adolescence to fifty-nine. One evening the conversation drifted to parenting. Out of curiosity I asked them about their father relationships. All seven, without exception, as they went around the group, indicated that *each* had lost his or her father in childhood, either through divorce, desertion, or death. Clearly this is important data. How important is hard to say. All suicidal persons have not lost their fathers in infancy and all who do lose their fathers in childhood are by no means suicidal. It set me thinking, however, about the relationship.

A study by Urie Bronfenbrenner, entitled "The Changing American Child," charted significantly lower scores on responsibility and leadership in middle-class adolescents whose parents were away from home for long periods of time.[1] The findings indicate that such children may lack ambition, seek immediate gratification, feel inadequate, be followers of their peer group, and resort to juvenile delinquency.[2]

Some Examples of Father Conflict

Most therapists are frequently confronted by situations in which fathering or the lack of it had a traumatic impact on the individual from various psychological angles. I would like to mention a few that impressed me.

1. *Theme: Kleptomanic efforts to restore childhood paradise lost through "oedipal seduction."*
A college-aged woman, bright enough to have gotten an

advanced degree in one of our better universities, was caught stealing a typewriter. Remanded to me by the police, we worked together once a week for more than a year. She was natively attractive but was often disheveled, keeping herself poorly groomed. Relative to her peers at the time, one might say that she "dressed herself down."

During our sessions together it became evident that her interest in stealing was only symbolically functional and more classically kleptomanic than typically criminal. She took things that, considering the risk, were often of very little value apart from their personal significance. (The typewriter was an exception.) Most were such objects as lipstick or other cosmetics, silk stockings, and other items that might be used to enhance her attractiveness. The contradiction between this theft style and the way she kept herself most of the time was striking.

She had had a rather idyllic, center-of-the-universe childhood for five years. She was dressed like a doll by her mother. Upon the arrival of her first sibling, a brother, she was abruptly displaced from her central role in the family and became envious of the attention shifted to her brother..

Her memories of the father at this time were powerfully focused around playing on his lap, sliding down his knees onto his stomach while he lay on the couch. On at least one occasion he had an erection, an event that embarrassed them both yet somehow came to the attention of the mother. She stressed the impact of this event on her own place in the family. After the episode, the mother began to ignore her dressing of the daughter, minimizing her attractiveness and shifting even more enthusiasm to the brother.

She made associations between the symbolic theft (as a groping for affection) and her desire to return to the idyllic period of childhood when she was the center of everyone's attention. After she integrated these insights and her self-esteem grew, there were subsequent favorable adjustments in her adult life.

Her situation reflects, I believe, a symptom picture of compromise between a self-demeaning, self-punishing guilty role (the risk and embarrassment of exposure) and on the other hand an impulse to gain affection and recognition, with a return to status by forced means.

One never knows how much fantasy intrudes on memory, but it was evident that the episode or episodes with the father (and the mother's negative response) constituted a nodal point for her. By means of her insight and growing self-acceptance, she was able to integrate the irrational quality of her stealing impulse and reexperience different self-affects.

2. *Theme: "I killed my father!"*

A young man in his middle twenties requested counseling. I never liked the clinical description "inadequate personality" because of its godlike innuendos, but that term comes to mind in respect to his appearance. His affect was schizoid, his personal relationships were tenuous and fragile, and he gave the impression of a kind of deadness. His appearance was that of a person in mourning. Eventually, it became evident that this was exactly his condition.

When he was about eleven years of age, his father died. It wasn't just the fact of his father's death, but the fact that he was angry with his father at the time and was wishing his father dead.

He could not remember going through a mourning process at the time, but he could recall a kind of dazed conflict with a conscious sense of guilt that he had caused his father's death by his wishing. Fifteen years later, he was still mourning. The therapeutic outcome was not ideal, and he continued to give the impression, although improved, of a person who was haunted.

3. *Theme: "I drove my father away."*

A very attractive young woman in her mid-twenties came for counseling. She was extremely bright but had very low self-esteem. She had been married, had several children, and was divorced by her early twenties. She worked at a clerical job and was given to rather extreme emotional cycles of elation and depression. Her poor self-concept was a marked contrast with some experiences of popularity as a high-school teenager before marriage. The early marriage to an unimaginative husband took her out of school and away from supportive peers. The early divorce left her bereft of confidence.

Childhood memories were of an absent father and being left home by a mother who had to work . . . memories of coming home from school and playing alone in an empty house. Pictures that she drew were of lonely, dejected children with tears in their eyes.

Her father, often absent on business, was fond of her and she of him. The mother divorced him when the girl was four. Over the years, the mother convinced the daughter that she had to get rid of the father "for the child's best interests." Later, the mother made her feel responsible for the father's having to leave. The girl came to believe that she had been too competitive with her mother and that the oedipal crisis resulted in the father's being driven away by her own affection. She felt a heavy load of guilt over the separation.

Gradually she overcame this false sense of guilt for what was her mother's doing and gained in self-esteem. She started college night school (surprising herself with honor grades), married again, and made a gratifying social adjustment.

4. *Theme: "My father, and all men, are clowns."*

A couple came for marriage counseling after a year of troubled attempts at relating. The wife was a tall, commanding-looking, and attractive woman, very intelligent and artistically gifted. She was articulate and quick in her responses. The husband, on the other hand, was somewhat shorter than she, emotionally less labile, reticent in speech, and gave a rather drab impression. They both made intelligent efforts to bridge the gap between them, but it was an affective distance that defied their intellectual engineering.

One climactic moment came when I asked them to take turns in a therapeutic exercise that I learned from Fritz Perls and had often found effective. Each took a turn initially listing at length whatever he or she found unpleasant or painful about the other spouse, beginning with the phrase, "It makes me angry when you . . ." One starts and continues until he or she can think of nothing else. Then it is the other's turn. When the negatives are all out, then each takes a turn listing what is appreciated beginning with the phrase, "It makes me happy when you . . ." The husband was able to name quite a few things that satisfied him and that he enjoyed in his wife. When her turn came, the wife started out, "It makes me happy when you . . ." Then there was a long, embarrassing silence. (She had been glib about the negatives.) The silence went on for several minutes as she searched for a way around this massive blocking. Finally, I felt the necessity to interrupt and to discuss with them the possible significance of the blocking. They became aware of the affective chasm between them. Eventually, she left the man and married again.

Her relationship with her father had been a very distant and hazy one. He too had left the home early and had been thoroughly downgraded by the mother. Men were made out to be essentially buffoons who could not be trusted. In one of the drawings that she occasionally brought along, she had painted a picture of a dream she had had in which she showed a bride and groom accompanied by a very prominent male clown. The conflict in herself and in her marriage centered around this yearning for a meaningful male relationship countered by this powerful imagery of a man as a being who is not to be taken seriously any more than her father. (Incidentally, the drawing of a dream-image of her mother showed the mother as a large bird, perching on her head with huge claws sunk into her skull.)

Homosexuality

Aside from these personal therapeutic experiences, evidence on the significance of fathers comes out in the data concerning homosexuality. This very controversial subject naturally raises issues that are too far-reaching to explore here. Nevertheless, I would just like to draw attention to a statement I heard recently by psychoanalyst Irving Bieber who teaches at the New York Medical College.[3] He said that he had never seen a case of homosexuality in a male who had a good and warm father-relationship, and he has worked with hundreds of cases of male homosexuality in depth therapy. He remarked that in every instance of male homosexuality, even independently of the kind of relationship with the mother, he had never seen a true homosexual who had not had a poor affectional relation with his father, one in which the father was absent or rejecting or in some way distant and cold. To him the crucial factor was the father's warmth and honest affection for the boy. If such is the case, Bieber believes the boy can survive distorted relations with the mother or aggressive, seductive approaches (even some transient experiences) on the part of males without becoming homosexual.

Aside from the highly contested nature of homosexual problems, most therapists could list counseling experiences with juvenile delinquents, personality disorders, and numerous other situations involving gaps or deficiencies in the father–relationship with the child. Fritz Redl in his writings has documented very carefully the superego distortions that occur in such children.[4]

Fathering: Has It a Unique Quality?

What is *fathering?* In a long struggle over the question of the basic roots of fathering, some interesting hints from the field of primatology turned up. Hans Kummer, a zoologist at the University of Zürich, recently showed me a color movie he had made in Ethiopia of a troop of Hamadryas baboons. He has lived with these animals off and on in the wild over a period of three years, studying their habits. It is suggestive, however tangential, to see what fathering is at this primitive prehuman level. Some of the following possibilities emerge:

Protection. The Hamadryas male is two or three times the size of the female and usually dominates a band of four or more females. When there is a threat of attack, the females line up in the "attack shadow" of the father. The males of a band will join together even to fight a much more powerful leopard if he threatens, interposing themselves between the troop and the attacker.

Food. Baboons in the region Dr. Kummer studies must forage over considerable distances for food and water. Typically, at the beginning of each day, a decision must be made about which direction to go. They have almost a voting procedure: a young male of the troop will get up and start off in a certain direction. He looks behind to see if others are following. If not, he stops. Then another young one tries it. Only when one of the older dominant males agrees and starts off after a young one will the whole troop follow. Wisdom and experience have won their place in the survival pattern.

Contacting Behavior (my label). The male baboon, much more than the female, does seem to roam and play more, at least beyond the troop boundaries. (Obviously he sees more of the countryside in the process and is better prepared for leadership in the kind of voting mentioned above.) Dr. Kummer writes:

> The primate male, in general, is more aggressive and more dominant than the female. He is more likely to leave the group and to migrate. . . . In play groups the ratio [of males to females] is about eight to one. While the males are out playing, the females often remain with the female adults of their family group. Sociographic analyses further show that male juveniles interact in larger groups than females, who mostly associate with one partner only. *Preliminary data based on the same methods reveal a similar pattern in human children.* [italics mine][5]

One cannot honorably jump very far with such data to the human scene, but it suggests already at this primitive level a male function of contact with the larger environment, an exploring of it in mobility, and a testing of its limits and possibilities through play interaction.

If *mothering* at the animal level involves a *turning inward* to the feeding of and caring for offspring, then *fathering* loosely generalizes in the direction of a *turning outward* toward the extended environment and its potential of food, shelter, and danger. To the extent that there is differentiation of function, it seems similarly organized between male and female in many animal and human groups.

Mother represents a focus of dependency and blood-tie. Kummer writes:

Nonhuman primates recognize only matrilineal kinship. The subgroup of a mother and her children shapes the latter's social relationships in three species investigated in this respect and presumably in many others as well. Chimpanzees preserve strong bonds with their mother and their siblings well into adulthood. The social rank of juvenile rhesus monkeys among their age group precisely corresponds to and depends on the rank of the mothers.[6]

This model of mother facing inward toward the family's needs and father being a kind of structuring contact with the outer world finds many parallels in human society, certainly in myth and in many psychological elaborations. The tie to mother is the tie to the womb, to nurturing dependency, to blood and origin, to mystery and unconsciousness, the immediacy of primitive vitality and continuity.

The tie to father is the tie to the one who calls away from the womb, from dependency, to the world "out there," the world of danger, of war, of food scarcity, of spatial boundaries protected or invaded, of rules for survival vis-à-vis other families, other tribes, other nations, and so forth. It is the tie to one who has roamed, played with, fought, and contacted what is out there, one who is conscious of and able to accumulate a lore and wisdom about the world.

By now those in the women's movement have a right to be enraged and deserve equal time. We do not wish to insult anyone, especially with baboon analogies. We will return to the support of these conceptions of fathering in a moment in respect to mythology. Before we do so, I would like to focus briefly on two psychologists as they conceptualize the core of fathering.

For Freud, fathering comes into sharpest focus in the third to the sixth years of life of the child. The oedipal conflict in the child is his first real struggle with a paradigm of society. It is a triangle. It is a conflict of love and hate, of affection and power. For the child, it is the question (not usually articulated as such): How do I get what I want (*i.e.*, the love of one parent) when someone is in the way (*i.e.*, the other parent with his or her prior claims)? At its most primitive emotional level, it is the question: Do I have to kill to get love? This is why Freud saw murder and incest to be the central core taboos of all moral systems. Normally the child answers this question by an emotional compromise: winning as much love as possible from both parents by identifying with the same-sexed parent and adopting the family rules and boundaries concerning love and power. (Freud, however, recognized a partial double identification with both parents.)[7] This is largely an unconscious and repressed problem that is worked out in the economy of anxiety reduction. Fathering, in this context, constitutes a patterning process through which, behaviorally and conceptually, conditions of community living are introjected, such that conflicts over love and power, inner wishes and outer necessities, may be resolved.

In his book *Ego Development and the Personality Disorders*, psychologist David Ausubel sees fathering as essentially a task of setting boundaries and limits to a child's ego expansiveness.[8] The small child, by virtue of his ability to get adults to respond to his cries and give him what he needs, has a normal tendency to develop a sense of omnipotence and to build much of his ego around his continually expanding sense of control of the world. At some point, which Ausubel thinks is usually around the age of two and one-half, this tendency toward omnipotence must be contained in order for a child to become a normal member of society. This is a psychological task usually focused in the father. At this age of what some call the "terrible twos" when the child's will must be in some sense confronted with reality, the process that Ausubel calls "satellization" normally sets in. By this term he means that the child surrenders his sense of omnipotence and moves from the implicit conviction "I am God" to the position "I am not God, but my father is. He is all powerful." If this transition does not take place in some form, we have as a result the typical character disorder or psychopathic personality who continues to construe the world as an extension of his own ego, rather than having distinct boundaries between what is his and what belongs to others. Thus we see the function of fathering oriented to this limit-setting role. This is not to say that there are not other ancillary and important aspects of fathering, but this is a critical focus.

If we are to summarize our discussion up to this point in respect to some of the possibilities intimated for fathering, we have, in addition to the primal significance of affection, protection, contacting behavior as a kind of modeling of the world relation or the relation with the surrounding environment, and *limit-setting*, which brings power to bear on the as-yet-unbridled expansiveness of the growing child.

Writing about this issue, Leighton McCutchen says, "The father figure is built upon a trialogue between the actual interrelations of child, father and mother as those come to focus on the problem of limitation and initiative."[9] He is calling our attention to the fact that *father* is a complex image that involves not only the actual father, but the father as he is perceived (partly in fantasy) by the child and as he is mediated and related to by the mother, directly and through her own memories of her father.

The Father in Myth

One of the best places to pick up the long-term human understanding of a psychological problem is mythology. I confess that in the midst of the violent confrontations and youthful rebellion of the last eight years I was hard put for a point of orientation until I came upon Erich Neumann's *Origins and History of Consciousness*.[10] He reminds us there that in almost all the mythologies of the ancient hero, such as Oedipus, there comes a time when the youthful hero's fate hangs on his violating the two central taboos of every culture: *murder* of the father and *incest* with the mother. If he fails, he is doomed to sterility or madness. This is a markedly strange inversion of the usual collective ethic. (I have drawn heavily, in this and the next several paragraphs, from a previous article of mine, "Guilt and the Now Man," published in *Humanitas*, Fall, 1969.)

The point of these strange myths, Neumann tells us, is to be found by interpreting the hero as a symbol of the ego in each one of us. When the child hero (ego) reaches maturity at the end of adolescence, he must "kill the father." Since the father represents traditionally the cultural canon—morals, justice, reason, and consciousness—this means that the hero-son must have the courage to stand against these if they violate life as he has come to understand it. Union with the mother represents his entering into his own unconscious, getting in touch with the creative feminine aspects (symbolized as anima) in his germinal inner core, out of which he may bring forth the new. By this and from this may come his contribution to the vital wholeness and completion of a next step in the growth of civilization, and individually, his own fulfillment. Only by this killing of the father (*i.e.,* breaking with the old canons) and merging with the mother (*i.e.,* exploring his creative unconscious), can the figure reach true individuation or become a hero, the hope of humankind.

Erik Erikson, who has weaned all of us in the social sciences on his conception of identity, notes the identity diffusion in many of today's young people and the difficulty of finding values that are stable or applicable enough to form a secure basis for identity—something that no doubt contributed to the mockery of serious values often noted and to the *now* quality of the impatience. As Erikson put it, "Every delay appears to be a deceit, every wait an experience of impotence, every hope a danger, every plan a catastrophe, every potential provider a traitor."[11]

Protean Man

Robert Lifton, a Yale University psychiatrist, feels that the concept of identity has been spelled out too rigidly and that we are seeing in young people today a movement toward what he would call "Protean man."[12] Proteus was the mythical Greek who could change his form at will—from boar, to lion, to fire, to flood, and so forth. What Proteus would not do unless seized and chained was to commit himself to a single form, the form most his own.

This Protean man, Lifton writes, "is starved for ideas and feelings that can give coherence to his world." He is obsessed with a "strong ideological hunger." He is sensitive to the absurdity and mockery of the older value systems and to a strong ambivalence about his dependency on older adults at the same time that he experiences anger about what he feels is an abandonment of him by them in his extremity.

Lifton believes that the superego may be disappearing somewhat in the classical sense, described as "the internalization of clearly defined criteria of right and wrong transmitted in a particular culture by parents to their children." He says, "Protean man requires freedom from precisely that kind of superego—he requires a *symbolic fatherlessness*—in order to carry out his explorations."

This would seem to suggest that where there is so much change and cataclysmic upheaval of values in the culture, it behooves those who represent the past (while being as clear as possible) to sit loose to the values that they are passing on to the younger generation, at least the *expectation* they charge them with. Clearly this emphasis depicts shifts in the process of fathering and a changing understanding of how it should work.

One can see such a dramatic shift in fathering evidenced in the story of Abraham and Isaac in the Old Testament. This story marks a crucial turning point in the Hebraic conception of the father–child relationship. Abraham was a dedicated believer in the midst of foreigners who measured their dedication by sacrificing their children to their god. We see in Abraham's struggle with this issue his conscience-demand taking him as far as the top of the mountain with his son and faggots of wood for the sacrifice. He went right up to the point where he was to slay his son, then "a voice" compelled him to stop and provided a substitute animal. If one takes this symbolically, it evidences a profound turning point in the superego and the restraints imposed on the parents by the collective value system, which up to that point had put the life of the child in the hands of the father, and substantiated the oedipal anxiety of the young with real examples of the father-killing of the child. This was a paradigmatic instance of love overcoming both fear and the powers invested by superstition. It was a real turning point in the elevation of the family and fathering in the Hebrew culture and in civilization.

Abraham is a father-hero—an example of the kind of mind so convinced of the ultimacy of love that it can challenge, out of its own ego autonomy (or, admittedly, possibly hallucinatory tension) and confidence in love, the demands of any code. One sees this emerging in some of the Old Testament prophets such as Hosea and in Job's questioning of God's ways and coming to full flower in Jesus, who finalized this evolution of the ultimacy of love.

Ego Morality and Fatherlessness

As two different theologically oriented psychologists, Oskar Pfister of Zürich and R. S. Lee of Oxford, have shown, this is a movement in both the fathering process and its internalization through superego identification from an authoritarian, code-oriented position (which says, "You do it because I told you to, and I'm stronger") to an ego morality (which says, "We do it because this is love, the condition of wholeness, community, health, reality"). It is not without authority, but it is authority that measures itself by reality and truth rather than by its own pride or muscle. In Erich Fromm's terms, it is authority based on competence (power to) rather than authoritarianism based on fear (power over). This is a shift in the psychodynamic base of morals from superego to ego. It is not a total shift, in that the affective dynamic of superego is still there, but even this becomes measured (as does the code) by the ego's relatively autonomous ability to assess reality. This has to happen in every person who "grows up" morally. It has to happen in any neurotic who wants to move to normalcy. It is now happening in theology as a major component of the "God is dead" phenomenon—man coming of age. It is a great deal of what has been happening among the youth of our time. The only real authority they now recognize (at their mature best) is competence, reality.

This has all been capsulized in recent writings as "fatherlessness." Mittscherlich has documented various ways in which western society is fatherless, such as the growing classlessness of mass man, the rejection of and hostility toward authority (with accompanying peer competition), the loss of reliable models in the environment (Watergate!), the father as clown or bumbler (recall our fourth patient's drawing), the splitting of the father's teaching role from his temperament (code from affect), alienation from "fatherland" (burning of flags, cynicism about patriotism, etc.). In brief, "the increase in specialization has led to fatherlessness of the first degree; to the loss of the physical presence of the working father, . . . to a general weakening of the primary object relationships. . . . Fatherlessness of the second degree dissolves the personal element in power relationships; one is aware of authority as event, but it cannot be visualized."[13]

I cannot easily forget a very illuminating personal vignette that occurred when I was in the throes of multiple early professional commitments and using most weekends to write a doctoral dissertation. My second son, then about five years of age, said one day to his six-year-old brother, "Let's play 'Daddy.'" I was all eyes and ears over what was to ensue. The younger one went into his bedroom, came rushing into the living room, grabbed my hat, slapped it on his head, frantically rushed around till he found my briefcase, then dashed out the front door, slamming it behind him. After that denouement, I slashed my way through my datebook and wrote in "family" here and there!

Systematic Fatherlessness

McCutchen raises the question of what happens when fatherlessness is systematically imposed.[14] He examines three models: (1) the kibbutz, (2) the American black family, and (3) children left with only a mother (by sickness, death, or divorce of the father).

In each instance, he finds deficiencies in the child. In

discussing the kibbutz he says, "The children seem emotionally flatter, less vivid people than their real parents. They
tend to be materialistic and prosaic, not spiritual or poetic
like their fathers." He calls attention to the primacy of peer
loyalty over family loyalty, diffidence toward ultimate
concerns and an aggregate cultural lowbrowism. In the
American black family confusion surrounds fathering. For
many a black child, *father* is multiple (he often *had* to stay
away for the family to survive), and the male appearance was
often forced to be furtive, militantly erotic, and sometimes
variable. Big Mama was "fatherized" and had to play all
roles. "The father figure is connected with militant procreation. That such a fathering should burst into the half-crazed
but telling rhetoric of the myth of Black Power should not
surprise us too much. The militants are recalling the nation's
shadow side, how it attempted to wipe out the generational
transmission of a cultural tradition through slavery."[15] As for
children with only a mother, in the case of younger children
who lose their fathers between approximately four to six (the
time of oedipal crisis and superego constellation), an intense
and detailed fantasy father tends to emerge, often endowed
with a greatly exaggerated sadism. It is as though the child
needed "not so much to be like the father, as to be a
father—someone to help limit his maternal ambivalence."
(His sadism *may* have special relevance to the suicide trends
we noted earlier in some who lost their fathers in childhood.)

McCutchen summarizes:

> If we draw together the lines of all three of these examples, the
> father figure embodies a complex system of meanings. These
> include: the direct *father substitute* of the communalized father
> where fathers are brothers, the child-like fathers of the black
> ghetto "baby," and the indirect *presence in imagination* of
> fathers for the fatherless children.

The stereotype of the father figure must be dissolved into a richer theoretical framework that can hold together these complexities without oversimplification. As long as the stereotype holds our attention, it seems that the father figure is on the wane. But if a richer analysis is used, the reverse interpretation may be the more fruitful one.[16]

I am convinced of the latter. Someone "fathers," whether the biological progenitor, a fatherized Big Mama, dominant peers, fantastic images, or some other surrogate.

It is my impression that kibbutz, black, and single-parent situations merely sharpen for us the intense need of the child for the living presence of a parent who, if not a father, is fully aware of the "fathering" functions defined above. Not only aware, but committed to modeling them for a child in a way that more and more enhances ego functions in moral decisions, while providing emotional companionship.

What the latter means is not easy to delineate briefly. At the very least, it suggests moving away from responses such as "Because I say so" or "Don't ask questions" toward "Here's why we believe it's best" responses, with logical and simple steps filled in where possible. It implies, too, that power and control of resources, though effective, should not be exploited as appeals to moral suasion but that reality, consequences, mutual decision-making, ego-identifying "we" language, and perpetuation of a studied fairness mentality (that occasionally also indicts the parental law-giver) all come into play.

It lies before us as an urgent and massive human problem to clarify further what fathering is, who can best do it, the extent to which nature is or is not superior to any substitutes, whether it is a function of cognitive–affective forces that can be separated from sex-typing without deleterious effects, and, if so, what constitutes its *sine qua non*. Civilization cannot lightly ignore this problem and be confident of continuing.

Chapter II

Our Father?

Theodore A. Gill

Reversing the Frances Thompson classic, Victor White suggests that when it comes to imaging God rather than defining him, God has long played Fox of Heaven to us pursuing hounds.[1] And of course, it is so. While we seek to snare the Fox, to seize him in a word, a title, a metaphor, he eludes us and races on before. We follow after, snuffling for his spoor, baying syllables into the cosmic bush, knowing that we never quite get him. But we keep trying

> down the nights and down the days;
> . . . down the arches of the years;
> . . . down the labyrinthine ways
> of my own mind; and in the mist of tears
> . . . and under running laughter.

Maybe not with unperturbed pace, but with a pretty majestic instancy, we seek the appropriate image for our "now you see him, now you don't" God.

The quest has been going on for a long, long time—since people have been able to ask questions at all, in fact. There seems to be little doubt now what shape some of the first humans came up with to visualize divinity or, better, to make the circumambient Mystery recognizable, addressable. That shape stands today for all to see in a Vienna museum, a precious relic found not too far from where it is now shown, protected by glass and who knows what electronic maze, guarded by the state, and close-wrapped in its own enigma.

In a day when it is hard to surprise anybody with anything, the religious studies teacher can still get a stir out of a college class when, after introducing the subject of the next slide ("Maybe the earliest known representation of divinity, Neolithic, *circa* 25,000 B.C.E. It was discovered in 1908 by a road workman in southern Austria"), the teacher throws onto the screen a huge image of the tiny, rockhard, bulbous Venus of Willendorf. "Why, he's a lady!" answers a student when pressed to verbalize his reaction to the ancient image of divinity, thus scrambling eons, perceptions, theologies, cultures, along with his pronouns.

And indeed, the Venus of Willendorf *is* female, about as female as a 4½-inch statuette could be. Big, unevenly pendulous breasts hang over the swollen belly couched in wide hips, with carefully delineated genital area. Everything else is thrown away; the legs are stylized into a split cone tapering off the bottom of the figure, the matchstick arms are sketchily modeled as if folded across the tops of the breasts, and the head—a curiously cobbled knob—bends forward somewhat diffidently.

Apparently, this overwhelmingly maternal figure was the very figure of divinity to those who sculptured her and all the other Venus figurines from her time, for there are many of her type in museums now. By their number, their original locations, and their similarities, we can safely conclude that they were made and preserved as ritual elements in religious worship of some kind. It is not convincing to suggest that hundreds of archaic artists, in little touch with one another,

suddenly began doing stony portraits of their mothers or
wives all at the same time. Nor is it probable that with the
same primordial spontaneity, legions of quasi-brute boys
chipped rocks into surrogate realizations or sublimations of
nagging incest ambitions. (Although, as Laurie Schneider
points out in her classroom lectures, the odd texturing over
the Venus of Willendorf's head could represent the caul that
always hides the mother's head in incest dreams—a sort of
last-gasp censoring of the inadmissible in the very act of
dream admission.)

It is more likely that we see in these Venuses confirmation
of the trusted nature of ultimacy long, long before conscience
is supposed to have dawned. Whatever else, whoever else,
was included in some Ice Age pantheon (of which we have
no clue), the cultists and devotees who moved to influence
the Unknown with their swollen little sculptures saw the
important part of that mystery as maternal. The marvelously,
lovingly fashioned figurines are limestone prayers:

> Our Mother, which art in heaven.
> hallowed be thy name.
> Thy kingdom come,
> thy will be done.

The "kingdom" was one of vegetative and animal plenty; the
"will" was obviously for fertility. Somehow, somewhere, in
the Nature of Things, there had to be a Grand Maternity back
of everything that mattered, and the earliest human beings
(marked as humans as much by the pathos of their hope as
by any other distinction) obviously lived in the hope that she
was available to their ritual approaches and responsive to
their primal urgencies.

How could the first faith and its imagery have been
otherwise for the earliest humans? A qualitatively new
species was being eased into its unique history—being
drawn like water-skiers up out of the pressing, penetrating,

supportive-resistant lake of nature where independent initiatives had been sluggish, suddenly to skim its surface, depending on that surface but free now to slide over it, to choose direction on it, to overleap it at will, to make history. As the qualitatively new species tried on its transcendence, was extended by its imagination, was able to wonder, what *could* it image behind all this newness except Woman, Mother?

Where did the first people see novelty coming into the world? From between the thighs of women, that is where. Stones could be chipped into knives and spearheads, and clay could be molded into pots, but that was the rearranging of existing elements. Where did they come from, those things no part of which had been here before? Where alone did radical novelty, the brand new, the unaccountable, enter the world and history? From the bodies of the females, of course, and unassisted: the causal connection between one day's paired spasms of delight and a much later day's lonely labor pains was quite unsuspected.

So, when we were first able to wonder about where everything had come from, we apparently extrapolated from our common experience the extraordinary, enormous Maybe, the naïve What-If that in unsophisticated minds elides noiselessly into Must-Be. The feminine is ultimate source; the Great Mother must be the maker of heaven and earth; all hail to her.

There is much evidence in the artifacts of that antiquity and in the reconstructible myths of the earliest stretches of human history to support this surmise. The Snake Goddess of the Minoans may be one of the loveliest and latest of the artistic evidences, but she and the Willendorf Venus stand at opposite ends of an eons-long continuum of devotion to the variously named Magna Mater.

Myths were changed as political, sociological, and

ecclesiastical developments dictated, but even in mythology in its final form, clear traces remain of the feminine principle's original domination of the divine.

Yet, after tens of thousands of years of passionate devotion to the Great Mother, for the last few thousand years men and women have, one way or another, prayed "Our Father . . ." The story of the conversion of theological conception and imagery is complex and still being pieced together. It is, of course, closely related to changes in the circumstances of human life and to the political and economic adjustments that paralleled those. But it is of special interest to Western religionists that apparently the weightiest, most strenuous, and most persistent challenge to the feminine theological dominance came out of the Arabian desert. It was the sinewy, black-bearded, patriarchal Semites (religious ancestors to Jews, Christians, and Muslims) who poured out of their rocky, scorched land—a kind of pressure cooker of religious conception—to insist upon the masculinity of all important authority, including that which they believed resided beyond their burning skies.

So we who live within the great Western religious traditions will look in vain for traces of the supposedly universal Great Mother in our sources. If she was ever there, her strata were carefully buried in Arabian sands before the Semites ever brought their powerful masculine offensive onto the world stage. Sweeping all before them, the desert people—renowned, admired, desired, feared among other peoples for their thrusting virility—seconded existing forces working toward a paternal divinity and initiated their own campaign to put a male god securely on the cosmic throne. As revised myths, art, and ancient history amply attest, they succeeded. Not just our God, but everyone's top god, is confidently patriarchal. The success of this enormous spiritual and cultural revolution is revealed in that until very recently it has been taken utterly for granted that it should be so.

Well, maybe not quite utterly. The Great Mother lost her place in pantheons all over the world, as great male gods dominated everywhere; they undoubtedly got the formal honors. But there is no doubt which divinities received the most passionate devotion of the people: the goddesses of love and fertility, the epochal daughters and granddaughters of the Great Mother. Well into the common era, the mystery religions, embraced by people weary of the perfunctory worships of the stately father gods, were most often formed around these imported goddesses with all the sexuality-maternity that clung to them from the earliest, deepest levels of human religious imagining. Isis, Ishtar, Cybele, Astarte, and Magna Mater herself were great cult figures during and after Jesus' time. In these figures, people continued to worship the vast germinal, nutritive, creative, supportive, rhythmical, receptive forces of nature—of Magna Mater. In the worship of a female deity that ranged from gracious austerity to orgiastic abandon, the people continued to affirm and identify with surging, visceral, fluid, repetitive, inevitable, natural reality. They accepted the life and the body and the world that the Great Mother gave them, reconciled themselves to her cyclical ways, and never completely disengaged from the chthonic womb whence they came and so were somehow ready to curl up in it again at the end. (Now we find their skeletons arranged in fetal position in oval tombs.)

No wonder the Mother worship appealed and would not down. It is a large part of essential religiosity. It makes you at home in the world, adjusts you to the family and furniture of existence, relates you to emergence and growth, connects you with the earthy vitalities, gives you a tenderness in which to confide and which you know will be fiercely for you

when necessary, and gentles you toward the dread final-
ities.

Our Father pulls against all of that. Whatever fathering
means psychologically and sociologically, theologically it
means the opposite of mothering. When divinity had been
transexualized and became thoroughly masculine, there was
none of the flesh-of-one-flesh identification in that male
imagery that comes with the extended gestational intimacy
of mother and child. The father's relation to his children's
genesis is momentary and expulsive. There is more of fiat
than total engrossment and slow nurture in it. Generation is
more a matter of spasm, spurt, and stand aside for the father
(however sedulous his husbandry) than it can ever be for the
mother in her long, mysterious creating of bone of her bone
and blood of her blood.

In theologies for which the master metaphor is male,
creation is indeed by fiat. The world's body does not begin
and go full term in God's body. Creation is something that
happens abruptly outside of divinity, and on independent
volition. That primal separation of Father God from his
creation and its creatures is basic and irrevocable in the
belief picture ruled by the masculine metaphor. However
theological sophistication may later gloss the fact with
doctrines of immanence, there is a fundamental over-
againstness about the father–child relationship that derives
from the masculinity of the base image of God.

It is all there in Michelangelo's creation panel on the
ceiling of the Sistine Chapel. Adam, languid on his
continent, raises an arm tentatively toward the Father
Almighty, whose authoritative arm stabs down toward the
dewy new man. Index fingers on both hands reach toward
each other, but *they do not touch.* All of the subtle, pervasive
implications of the patriarchal Judeo-Christian symbolization of God tremble in the air between those outstretched

fingers. Father and child reach out to each other, but they do not touch. There is a space between them that, because of the biological elements in the maternal metaphor, is inconceivable in the earlier religions of the Great Mother.

The Father and his children are everlastingly viś-à-viś. Separate integrities are guaranteed. Infinite qualitative distinctions are not to be smudged or smothered. Absorption of one in the other, or of one in the Other, is not in the picture. Union is out; communion is the most that is desirable or possible.

The twentieth-century fascination with Martin Buber's I–Thou formulation is instructive. It is assumed by many that the hyphen is connective. It binds the I and the Thou in a personal subject-to-subject encounter. People whose stated religion centers on a Father—people yearning for an intimacy with the originating reality denied them by their central image—impute umbilical significance to the hyphen. Obviously or surreptitiously, by design or by accident, these persons hope that the hyphen unites what was once One, what never was separated, and what must finally be One again.

The intention and religious genius of the I–Thou design, however, runs in the opposite direction. The hyphen, which does hold the disparate parties in confrontation, is also a bar holding the parties off from more than encounter, from more than a mutual recognition of quite separate, individually responsible integrities. The hyphen does not bond; it defines the space between. It is the same space Michelangelo painted. The Jew, Martin Buber, the New Reformation Christian teachers who capitalized on his insight, and the Renaissance Catholic artist were all completely faithful to their Father.

The pointing finger of the Father (and sometimes a finger is only a finger) does not latch onto his child's hand; he does not coerce the child, drag the child into contact, or haul the child into his own orbit. The Father's finger stays free for all the other gestures appropriate to father–child relationship in the patriarchal picture. The finger summons, points directions, commands, warns, cajoles, admonishes, accuses, shames, sends away. The two distinct autonomies remain inviolate; the Father assumes the child's responsibility, establishes boundaries, judges, rewards, punishes. So it was, apparently, in the desert tent; so it would be under heaven.

Certainly in Christian theology when the doctrine of God the Father is handled, it is predominantly in terms of God as Creator and God as Lord. These are the vigorously objective synonyms for Father in both Jewish and Christian traditions of teaching. No wombed divinity here, rolling with the cyclical rhythms the Great Mother knew in herself, source of whatever she created, source of the observation of, acceptance of, and participation in the pathos and irony of her close-held creatures' lives; source of their anticipation of endless renewals and beginnings again. Instead, God the Father (as Creator) breaking and bending out the great hoop of history, stopping its incessant rolling (what does the Father know of cycles in himself?), stretching time from God's own here to there, and setting his fractious creatures on their once-and-for all intrusive, manipulative, guilty-aspiring, highly dramatic way. And from the beginning, to climax, to end, of the single track, God the Father (as Lord) is in charge. Creatures charged by the Father-Creator to "dominate and subdue" the creation, do so under the command, challenge, correction of Father-Lord. And ever and always the Father's majestic and magnificent demand that his children do right by him by doing right by each other.

The point is not that Our Mother worship was tenderer

because women are tender and Our Father worship is tougher because men are tough. The premises are too doubtful and the practices too complex to be so syllogistically comprehended. The Father-Creator-Lord of Judaism, for instance, loved mercy as well as justice—he is the shepherd who makes me to lie down in green pastures and restores my soul and is with me, yea, though I walk through the valley of the shadow of death; he yearns after his people as Hosea longs for his harlot wife; he continuously rescues his nation from exile in whatever remnant. Although God is often Householder, Employer, Rich Man, he is also Shepherd, Father of the prodigal (which for its truest tenderness should be seen in the balletic exegesis of Prokofiev-Balanchine),and Father of Jesus Christ, who insisted that God the Father is love even while he, the Son, was obedient to the Father's terrible demand.

The point simply is that Our Mother worship and Our Father worship are different. The older religion is the more mystical, features accommodation with nature and event, and has its more fateful aspect. The supervening religion—the one with which we are most familiar—is fundamentally ethical, expects confrontation with nature and events, and is robustly voluntaristic even when unimpressed by "works."

Interestingly, the religions of a Father God have always indicated in their development that another aspect of divinity was not being given sufficient place (or, more dramatically, that the Great Mother has never given up and is always finding ways to press her continued claim). For instance, when goddesses were worshiped in the great desert, long before the Father God usurped all honor, human bloodlines were appropriately traced through the mother rather than the father (as in the much attended geneology of Jesus of Nazareth). That tradition is just a trace of the oldest religious world, but it is a trace that lingers still. To this day,

according to the patriarchal rabbinic law, a child's Jewish-
ness is dependent on the bloodline of the mother.

May there not be another such trace of an earlier order in
the high place historically accorded the Jewish mother within
the formally patriarchal family? Thanks to her literary sons in
twentieth-century America, her generic group has lately
been clawed at, cried over, and laughed down. But at her
best, she is hailed in the Talmud as God's answer to his
problems with omnipresence: since God had trouble being
everywhere all the time, he made mothers to be his local
surrogates, delegating some of his creativity to them. The
concession comes as a jolt within Judaism, unless one
remembers the profound historical depths of the soil in
which all religion grows.

If tentativity is held before us like a shield, we may
advance at this point the conjecture that circumcision—far
from being the token of castration by the father or the gesture
of penis envy by the mother, as classic psychoanalysis
regards this intimate mutilation—may still be in its present
depths what it once might have been in the past: a bloody,
once-only approximation of that cyclical blood flow of the
female regarded atavistically as concommitant with the
woman's mysterious power to create and produce a new life.
In the religious rite of circumcision, blood flows, a part of the
indubitably male excrescence is excised, and the penis in its
new configuration is born. Bruno Bettelheim, developing the
proposal with great richness of allusion, subtitles his
Symbolic Wounds, "puberty rites and the envious male."
Again we hear the whisper of a time when Mother was in
charge and men were ill-equipped in what matters most. In
awe and fear, they sought by ritual to identify with the
feminine power whose primacy was so long taken for
granted. (*Couvade* was once widely practiced and is still a
custom among some remote South American tribes, where

men are treated as if pregnant when their wives are and "lie in" through their mutual labor. The dead seriousness of such ritual simulations cannot be questioned.)

Of course, if this accounting for circumcision does not finally hold up, the more traditional explanations mentioned in the last paragraph fit as well in the religious world where a triumphant, all-powerful Father God calls for the subduing and dominating of the Mother's earth. Conjectured depth jealousies and/or envies quite aside, circumcision can be viewed as an uninvited, unresisted, irreversible taking-issue with the summary of the world's long process that each body is at birth. In another light, circumcision is the most precise sacrament possible for the aggressive Father's putting the mark of masculine, handmade history on nature's receptive, developing, cumulative being.

In Christian history, too, the feminine remains close beneath the masculine surface of the faith. The Church itself, biblically identified with the body of Christ, shades also into the bride of Christ. Plot lines tangle in Wagnerian confession when shortly the institution is also Mother Church (even for the notably unsentimental Calvin, Church was Mother). In Christian art, the great round, fructifying earth as a whole is as much a symbol for the Church (which is still also the body of Christ, who is the Second Person of the Deity) as the plump and seedy pomegranate. The ardent devotion to the Virgin Mary is another evidence of the instinct for a maternal centering, quite unengaged by our Father and the religion he dominates, that finds and develops disproportionately the congenial elements detected within the main teaching. In Eastern Orthodoxy there is the important place given to Sophia—wisdom, rationality, the feminine capacity shared by God and human beings making our correspondence possible. In recent centuries, American Protestantism has unconsciously (one must hope) and clumsily redressed the metaphorical balance by lacing its hymnology with maidenly turns of phrase and sighing sounds, and by portraying Jesus with embarrassingly misplaced femininity.

But then in the long-ago female theological ascendency, there must have been advised and ill-advised efforts to correct that metaphoric imbalance too. For the fact is that ultimacy must be beyond gender, as it is beyond conscience, and for the same reason. To be ultimate it must not only choose sides, it must not even be sided. We may prefer a partial; we may be devoted to a partial; but insofar as partials presuppose a whole, profound religion must save its deepest commitment for the enigmatic One—the One beyond symbolization who offers us options of insight on which to exercise our symbolizing powers, between which to activate our ability to decide, and around which to organize our lives.

Just as God is beyond gender, God is not unisex; neither is God androgyne. We simply must stop writing our tedious categorizations on the clouds. God is an ineffable whole of whom human beings, both male and female are true images, wonderful for their commonality and glorious for their polarity. We men and women, spotted so individually and so variously on the sexual continuum, are signs in ourselves of the dense and complex abstractness of our God—of whom we *all*, leaning this way and that as we do, are somehow images.

So our theological and devotional imagery will not label deity either as father or as mother, but as both. This will not, it is to be hoped, mean the rewriting of classics of any kind. That is a historical arrogance and an artistic blasphemy we should not add to religion's already abundant aesthetic sins. But in new theological and liturgical writing, the rich complexity of reality must find fairer representation than it has in the last thousands of years. If adding the older mother symbol to the newer father symbol jars some for a while, and if we do not think it is our Christian duty to be contemptuous of less sophisticated sensibilities than our own, perhaps variations on the undifferentiated parent image could be used more frequently.

But finally, our God must be both Father and Mother. God can no longer be either one or the other. Not just metaphysical and ontological sophistication is involved here, or even spiritual wholeness, but our earthly physical fates. However plastic the images of human maternity and paternity are right now to the pummeling and kneading of both theories and realities and however altered our conceptions of each will finally come to be, there are atavisms and primordial perceptions involved that will continue to shape people's understandings and expectations unless, alas, social liberations accomplish one vast historical lobotomy. Right now we need both of those perceptions with the responses appropriate and pendant to each.

The beauty and wholeness of the earth, the health and survival of the children of God, depend upon a new attitude toward nature. We may still debate the various historical and philosophical analyses of our problem on an abused planet, but there is no arguing that something about our attitude toward the world has permitted Western peoples to strip and gouge and foul their home sphere until not just beauty, but life itself, is threatened. If, as has been learnedly suggested, the religious bases of our vital perceptions have been skewed from the start, then Judeo-Christian believers must look again at their basic imagery. And if it then turns out that there is more precious significance in that casual dust of which we all were formed than we had noticed—we who have put all our attention on our mighty Father's wet issue that moistened the essential dust into modeling clay—we must be ready for theological reenvisionings. There may be more in Mother Nature than we have noticed when we invoke her, as we customarily do, with a shrug to justify some new irresponsibility of ours. Through her and the cellular potentiality of her vast body, we are bonded—all creatures and all creation, bone of her bone and flesh of her flesh into a family. There are problems, of course: Mother Nature and Mother God may not be identical. The leafy mysticism that trembles in the air whenever nature gets heavy emphasis does not always appeal. Even so, our Mother and our devotion to her is now of the most instantly practical salvific significance. Through her and the intimate identification we have in her with all that is threatened, familial affections may operate from inside us to hold the rapacious claw, joining the more exterior logical and legal restraints on our falsehood.

Death, too currently studied with such grimly cheerful determination and thoroughness, may also find a more natural fitness when the figures of both parents are included in the religious consciousness. Theological sophistication has long known that mortality is part of our creation; our physical obsolescence is built in. Knowledge of that fact is a prime token of our transcendence. Knowledge of that is at the root of both our misery and our grandeur as human beings. The same anxiety that leads us to prideful excess also conduces to our glorious creativity. When the Great Mother ruled men's imaginations, there was no doubt that death was as natural as life. The grief of loss was as great, but the terror, the resentment, that complicates our grief would not be there. There was little place then for the bewildering sense of the deceased's being hustled into the inaccessible chambers of an incomprehensible criminal justice system. *That* came on powerfully with the Great Father and with attendant misunderstandings. The early artists who gave us our familiar image of the patriarchal deity did not themselves doubt for a moment that death is part of the natural, created order. They had that from the Mother mythology in which they grew up. But their careless interpreters, carried away with the terms of responsibility, obedience, transgression, judgment, and punishment that moved forward with the Father, subsequently lumped death along with labor and its pains as part of the retribution of our exacting Father. (It is interesting that the same misreading of the Bible that makes death a punishment, when in biblical times it clearly was natural, also makes labor natural, when it clearly was once a punishment.) Whatever comes of our theological re-visioning, attitudes toward death cannot help becoming more wholesome as both Parents settle into our conception.

And it must be both Parents. Overzealous redressment of balance is the surest way to new imbalance. The Father, with all the sense of structure and direction that attends his image, is essential to the whole picture. He may have come late in mytho-poetic history, but he had to come. The strain that his expectations put on us exercises our humanity. The anxieties that his goals and supervisions may raise in us also charge and stretch our creativity. There is, no doubt, irony in the Mother's gaze as she observes the Father's children wrenching nature into the fugitive lineaments of history while her endless seasons roll. But there is an equally significant pity (contempt?) in the Father's eye when it falls on human potentiality that will not crack the womb, will not try its transcendence, will not take the fleeting glory.

Finally, it is aesthetic consideration that commands the double vision. In human life as in theological speculation, however the equities and amenities are worked out between masculinity and femininity, distinctly different mother and father models and images must be identified. Otherwise, there is no texture to our reflection or to our living. Without variety we are without choice and without choices we are without humanity. Variety is under concentrated attack now.

Technological, political, educational, commercial, even ecclesiastical developments threaten to mash us toward the ultimate homogenization, in which human being jells, until—on a forseeable morning—there is no more point in getting up.

Variety is not the spice but the source and context of all. Then life lived under a richly textured divinity may itself have texture and tension, may be stretched arrestingly on a web of multiform reality, may again be worth our while.

Chapter III

The Search for Paternal Roots: Jungian Perspectives on Fathering

Ann Belford Ulanov

Jung's theory of depth psychology is distinguished by its emphasis on the unconscious as an objective reality, exerting specific pressures on our subjective consciousness, producing as it does so compensating viewpoints and directions of development. The unconscious does not determine consciousness in a fixed way, but it operates constantly in the background. Nevertheless, its existence needs to be acknowledged, positively demands to be. Jung articulated his observation of the psyche's objectivity and its effects on our conscious identities in his theory of the archetypes, seeing the archetypes functioning in our psyches as ready-made forms or possibilities of behavioral and emotional response activated by concrete life situations.[1]

In the grip of archetypes, we feel ourselves caught by a force larger than ourselves, accompanied by clusters of images that we come to recognize as falling into certain unmistakable types. We register this kind of event as one of the deep human experiences of our lives.

One such important experience is that of having a father, not just physically but psychically. Our images of what a father is or might be, Jung says, are influenced by our experience of our actual father, of persons who acted toward us as father surrogates, and of the plentiful images of father figures in our culture. Our unconscious introjection of those father images assures that their influence will continue to operate in our adult lives long after we have ceased to be children. Damaged images and painful experiences of the father also live on in us unconsciously like a bruise that does not heal and that makes us continually vulnerable to fresh woundings. It is precisely to repair such damage that many people seek the intervention of psychotherapy.

In addition to biographical and cultural factors that help make up the father image operating in our psyches, Jung theorizes that our personal image of the father is unconsciously influenced by the father archetype in which the general human experience of fathering is compounded. Thus our subjective personal notion of "my father" has in its background an objective, impersonal image of "the father" that is called into play by what happens or fails to happen in our conscious experience of father. Hence, when Jung talks about the "father imago" and its influence in our lives, he means three things: our conscious concepts and images of what a father is, influenced in large part by memories of experiences with our own fathers and father surrogates; our unconscious introjection of how we saw our fathers when we were children, which often is at variance with the person our father actually was, a mixture of distorting projections and accurate perceptions; and the archetypal images of the father set into play by our own experiences.[2]

The Father Archetype

The father archetype consists of a cluster of images and associated behavioral and emotional possibilities of response that together convey the human picture of what "father" is and what it stands for symbolically. First among these is father as procreator, prime mover, begetter of new being.[3] In contrast to the tangible material birth process associated to the maternal, the engendering activity of the father is characterized as intangible and invisible, rather more a spirit than a human person. Frequent symbols of this father spirit are the wind, the voice, the spermatic Word, the life breath that enlivens the soul and takes it beyond the limits imposed by the body.[4]

The very invisibility of the sort of spirit associated with the father brings with it certain vulnerabilities and dangers. For example, one can easily mock this "spiritual" activity as entirely imaginary, especially if one contrasts it with the palpable fleshy activities of the feminine—conception, pregnancy, and birth. And then there is the equally dangerous temptation involved in the use of this kind of "spiritual" language, to drift off into abstractions and impossibly generalized speculations, altogether forsaking concrete connections to real persons and events. But none of this should make us forget the special values that come with this reading of fathering. For in it the father has been associated symbolically with a particular kind of consciousness that is uniquely capable of discrimination between self and other. It is a form of consciousness that enables us to stand back from instinctual processes happening within us and to conceive of an individual identity or ego development without falling into the archaic collectivity of the impersonal unconscious.[5] It is because of this experience of ego differentiation that the father is sometimes symbolized as the very *principium individuationis*.[6]

The father as a symbol of consciousness extends to general cultures as well as to individual persons. In mythology, for example, the king as father of his realm usually represents the dominant type of ego-consciousness reigning at any given time in any given society. He stands for the ordering principle operating within that particular culture, asserting the collective values of his civilization. The king's association with divinity underlines the supreme value of egoconsciousness and its creative powers.[7]

The oft-repeated fate of kings in mythological stories—that they die and a successor must be found among their sons or that they are ailing and must be regenerated—points to transformation rites that are peculiar to the father archetype and to the way in which this archetype finds its renewal in relation to the son. The father represents the wisdom of tradition, "the precious acquisition of our forefathers, namely the intellectual differentiation of consciousness."[8] In the guise of the "wise old man," another persistent archetype, the father instructs the son figure in the traditional ways of the spirit that are embodied collectively in the culture's dominant religious, philosophical, or educational systems.[9] In this archetypal guise, a father communicates to the young the spirit by which one can live, the truth that inspires and guides the life-giving activities.

The authority of the father finds constant renewal through being projected and embodied in different symbolic forms and persons chosen, consciously or unconsciously, to fit different historical and societal conditions. Traditional wisdom thus continues to live through its reembodiment in fresh forms that every younger generation gives to values passed on from a previous generation. The spirit of paternal authority is by its nature formless and relative, "an expression of the mysterious dynamic of life itself" that finds ever fresh concretization in the fluctuating development of values within the group.[10]

The historical and relative nature of the father figures who embody the father archetype is clearly illustrated by one of its negative manifestations. Instead of begetting and inspiring the development of consciousness, the negative side of the father thwarts it by a tyrannous refusal to give up power and make way for the son, as the world's literature, folktales, and dramas constantly remind us. Instead of yielding to the process of transformation, the negative force of the fathers blocks further development of consciousness or pushes it in the wrong direction, insisting on rigid adherence to the old values. Some of the pervasive malaise of our present culture arises from a split between fathers and sons typified in the opposition of the so-called establishment and the radical counter-culture. A father may capture and then destroy his son's consciousness by refusing to support its independent development. He feels any innovation of the son as a betrayal. He may have so concretized the values of his own generation that they have become petrified relics for him. If his son complies and identifies totally with his father, he becomes "bound by traditional morality," as Erich Neumann puts it, "castrated by convention."[11] At the opposite extreme, a father may fail to represent and pass on the legacy of his culture's values to his young. He then falls victim to an exaggerated formlessness that concretizes nothing and leaves his children no guidance by which to take their bearings.

If a son is too firmly identified with the formless invisible penetrating spirit of consciousness, he loses touch with the other side of his masculine spirit, which is expressed in the body and the unconscious in the blunt terms one finds in the male force in nature. The father archetype is also symbolized by such natural forces as the heat and the blazing light of the sun that warms the earth and in human terms shows itself as an emotional ecstasy that seizes consciousness, breaking in upon it and lifting it well beyond itself. Thus if a man identifies one-sidedly with the celestial aspect of spirit, living in the name of clarity at a distance from the natural cycles of the body, he loses his roots in the earthy side of the masculine spirit. He is cut off from access to the unconscious and cut off too from any strong or significant assertion of his sexuality and aggressive energy. Such an unbalanced development will produce a masculine identity that may be lucid but is also pallid and without emotional vitality. The estrangement from a natural maleness may also appear in its opposite form, where a man falls victim periodically to seizures from the unconscious that manifest themselves as possession by unconscious affectivity through crude bursts of sexuality or aggressive rage that obliterate all consciousness of what is happening to him.

Although Jung strongly emphasizes the archetypal backgrounds of consciousness, he stresses just as much the role of life circumstances that evoke our latent archetypal dynamisms. Thus for him the intrapsychic dimension is matched by the equally important interpersonal and world dimensions that call the archetypes into play and upon which the archetypes must depend for their release. If we suffer the loss of a father, for example, not only do our external lives show impoverishment, but fundamental, if buried, psychic factors do not sufficiently emerge, leaving the soul as wounded as the deprived consciousness.

Two Men Who Lost Their Fathers

The following two descriptions illustrate the effects of the loss of a father on a son's psychic development. For each man, the father archetype was not sufficiently embodied because of early loss of the father, through death in the first case and divorce in the second. Each son suffered great psychic difficulty in experiencing the emergence of his ego from his unconscious and in developing the clear conviction that he would be able to live securely rooted in himself, that is, connected to his unconscious. Each man felt alternately cut off from the unconscious or submerged in it.

The experiences of these two men also illustrate the startling fact of the objectivity of the psyche, a fact upon which Jung places much emphasis. Just as the father archetype does not exist independently of life circumstances like a psychic mechanism that goes into operation automatically, but rather depends on the stimulus of interpersonal experience for its evocation in a person's life, so do life circumstances depend on psychic factors to complete them. In a deeply damaging situation, where a boy loses his father by death or divorce, the damage is not necessarily irreparable. Not only can a new father figure reevoke the father archetype, but the autonomy of the archetype can also press for its own completion, constellating situations in which the broken psychic connections may be rejoined and allowed to develop in their own appropriate way. Thus the healing process may work simultaneously from within as well as from without. This joining of inner and outer energies to assuage and repair the terrible pain of psychic wounds and to nurture growth typifies the comforting aspect of the spirit often associated with the father archetype. Jung compares it to the action of the Comforter of Scripture, to God's Spirit: "The Holy Ghost is a comforter like the Father, a mute, eternal, unfathomable One in whom God's love and God's terribleness come together in wordless union."[12]

The Case of Simon S.

Simon S., a middle-aged man, was only five when his father died suddenly from a heart attack. The family was abruptly forced to move back to Europe from the distant tropical country where they had been living. Europe was then in the midst of the travail of World War II, so that as a small boy Simon suffered multiple traumas simultaneously: the death of his father, the leaving of his home in a warm colorful climate for the cold winter of Europe, and the emotional chaos of war. Simon was the only boy in his family, with two older sisters and one younger one. He said that as a child he often felt left out of the family, unable to be an intrinsic part of his sisters' games or the female world they shared with their mother. Simon experienced his mother as rigid and undemonstrative emotionally except for occasional outbursts of rage that only made him feel guilty and frightened. He sensed he could not really touch his mother who "hated to be mussed up." His mother never remarried.

Before his father died, Simon felt rejected by him. He remembered his father as a man accomplished in his profession, of reserved temperament, with little expression in him either of anger or affection. In contrast, Simon thought of himself as a dreamy, curious boy, full of fantasy and feeling. Simon thought as a child that his father did not like his fantasy play with dolls or animals, frowning on it as effeminate. When his father died Simon felt he now must try to be the "man of the family." But as he saw it he failed miserably to fulfill this aspiration. When the family reached Europe they were often on the run and forced to hide from the enemy in their war-torn country. Simon often succumbed to dreadful panic in the face of constant bombing and recurrent death. He was ashamed of his fear, interpreting it as proof of his own inadequacy and helplessness to "protect" his family in a manly way.

Simon S. originally entered therapy in his thirties, with a male analyst, out of fear he was schizophrenic. He saw himself as a bundle of split-up parts, drawn simultaneously in homosexual and heterosexual directions and cut off from most feeling, yet periodically possessed by moods of despair or of soaring giddiness and manic inflation. He thought of himself as a highly rational person who could analyze situations logically, yet he longed for some more immediate involvement with life. But any opportunity for emotional involvement with another person simply flooded him with panic. He worked with his first analyst to good effect; he felt stronger and more stable in himself as a result. He chose then to work with me on the feeling and sexual issues that he felt still eluded him. We worked together for two years in both individual and group sessions.

During our work, Simon reported a striking series of images and fantasies that came upon him autonomously. These, he felt, perfectly symbolized his distress. One dominant fantasy theme was mixed with the memory of the boat trip his family took from his tropical homeland to Europe. He felt haunted by his vision of the land slowly disappearing, slipping away from the boat and from him. He saw himself standing alone on the deck, watching the colors of the trees and the ground slowly disappear in the distance. Around him, as far as he could see, there was nothing but endless water and the approaching coldness of the northern climate they were sailing toward. His mother was confined to her cabin with his sisters comforting her. His father's body was in a coffin somewhere on the boat. He was all alone, without even a toy. He remembered being dressed in girls' stockings that had been borrowed as some protection against the cold; he had no winter clothes of his own because he had lived all his young life in a hot climate. This fantasy memory embodied for Simon all his feelings of being cut off from life, sailing alone, feeling homeless, with no clear connection to any other person or to his own identity.

Simon's second fantasy series presented itself in two forms, in a set of images of his own body and one of images of a bird. He saw his body in his imagination as half-dead, half-alive. Divided along a north–south axis, his right side was healthy and manly and often colored black, to which Simon associated the deep color, vitality, and instinctive health of the black persons he had grown up with in his now foreign homeland. His left side appeared as shriveled, inert, a pallid white in color, all but dead. To this side he associated his European nature, his rationality, his civilized personality. His fantasy birds were similarly polarized and frustrated, birds capable of soaring high and yet unable to fly because of a crippled wing. The birds too were sometimes colored half-black, half-white. Simon felt these fallen creatures depicted his broken faith in life and his broken spirit. In speaking of them he often broke down into painful sobbing, which like the birds, was in strong contrast to his usual cool rationality. The grief Simon felt over his father's death and the painful lost relationship to just about every area of his own life overwhelmed his usual cool rational language and accompanying poise. Crying for Simon was not a cathartic relief but a way of losing his safe perch of rationality to fall headlong into the depths of his unassimilated pain.

It was with surprise and pleasure that both Simon and I greeted a new fantasy image that appeared close to the end of the two years we worked together. The image expressed the slow forging of connecting links he had achieved to his undigested pain and the natural life of the unconscious that lay behind it. The new bird image was of a plump, somewhat pedestrian bird that was dappled in a mixture of black and white. Simon liked this fat creature, felt comfortable with it, and was somewhat amused by its fitting combination of his two "sides." It was a creature of the air yet could walk on the ground. Its color joined black and white and what they symbolized, the instinctive and rational aspects of his own spirit, as well as his associations to his childhood and his acquired European culture. That it made him laugh suggested he was less identified with his pain and less defended from it, less impelled to keep his distance. He could laugh a little more at himself, thus gaining some compassionate perspective on his experience.

Simon chose to end our work when he decided to leave his home in America to return to Europe. One aspect of this present journey was a sense he now had of actively reenacting his long-ago childhood trauma of the boat trip. Before leaving America our last sessions dealt with the uprush of memories of that boyhood journey. But this time Simon imaginatively added something new to that trauma. He saw himself now, as an adult man, joining that little five-year-old boy on the boat deck and standing with him affectionately. He felt he had repaired some of his psychic injuries by embodying in the present some of the needed fatherly care and concern for that abandoned boy who had existed so long in a split-off state in his psyche. By connecting himself to his unconscious pain and bit by bit trying consciously to suffer it through and digest it, he was no longer unconsciously identified with it or with the abandoned little son. Simon now began to embody some of the father's side of the father–son archetype, reaching in a loving fatherly way toward the part of himself that had gotten stuck in a little boy's pain. Freed from fixation, that left-out dissociated part of his psyche could now begin to grow up to the age and fullness of life of the rest of him.

The Case of Tom W.

Tom W. entered therapy when middle-aged. He chose to work with me because he had read my book.[13] He said in our first session he wanted therapy because he felt strangely blocked: "Something holds me back, as if all of me was not living." His first dream after that session was of his father who was then dying of cancer but was denying the gravity of his condition:

> I was talking intimately and tenderly with my father. His condition of terminal cancer was known to both of us openly. We seemed to be reminiscing about the good old days. Then suddenly I saw his face full in front of me as it looked thirty years ago. He said, referring to his present physical condition, "It's too bad we can't wrestle right now like we used to." My reaction was total agreement.

Tom was ten when he lost his father, the exact age the dream recalled to him when it depicted his father's face as it had looked thirty years ago. His father had left his mother at that point, thirty years ago, for another woman and had not seen Tom or his younger sister in any of the intervening years. The first contact Tom had had with his father after that long period was just at the beginning of our work together. His dying father had asked to see him.

Before his parents' divorce, in the first ten years of Tom W.'s life, he said he had felt closer to his father than to his mother. He had many fond memories of sitting on his father's lap or rubbing his face against his father's whiskery cheek. He remembered his father singing to him. Yet he also remembered that he "feared his father's world" and felt his father pushed him too fast sometimes. One such time his father wanted him to put on boxing gloves and fight with him. Tom remembered he did not want to fight, but he finally agreed and struck out at his father, who was in a stooping position to match his son's height. He knocked over his father, who responded with anger, while his mother stood by laughing. Tom had many memories of his mother laughing at his father or in some way making fun of him or indicating that he was ridiculous. He felt shame on remembering how often he was drawn into joining with her in mocking and scorning his father. The tension between his parents grew, especially after his father lost his job and was unable to find another during the time of the depression. In many ways he felt that his mother had driven his father away, letting herself get fat, using foul language, being unfeminine and unladylike in comparison to the mothers of his friends. When the divorce came, Tom remembered his mother saying over and over with recurrent panic, "This can't be happening to us," and, with that memory, the fact that she slept half the day. It seemed to Tom "as if there were a hole in the bottom of me and all the sand fell out." He felt his mother's sense of defeat very keenly when they had to move in with her mother and live there in two rooms, he the only male in a household of grandmother, mother, and sister.

In his adult life, Tom suffered certain recurring difficulties. One of the most frequent was a feeling of humiliation. He often reviled himself for being "dumb," which did not mean stupidity so much as being unconscious of something happening of which he should have been fully conscious. For example, in treatment with me in both individual and group work, if I said something or if someone in the group said something that Tom did not immediately understand, he felt panic flooding him as if once more he was being "dumb." He mutely endured this attack of self-judgment at first without telling the other group members. Then he would drowse off and even fall asleep. The hostility this behavior aroused in others led to their challenging him. We soon got at what was behind this sinking into unconsciousness. He felt he should have known what was going on, or should not have needed whatever interpretation I came to make. He should have been conscious. He resented the fact of the unconscious, that it existed at all. He recalled his boyhood resolution to take care of his mother, grandmother, and sister now that he was the only man in the family, knowing at the same time he was too little to do so. Similarly, whenever the grown-up Tom experienced a number of conflicting emotions at once; he felt humiliated and angry at the confusion that came over him. His falling asleep both provided escape from his painful perplexity and expressed his anger at those persons who aroused conflicting feelings in him. He simply tuned them out.

Another problem of which Tom complained was feeling "disconnected." Sexually, for example, his lovemaking was interrupted by an inexplicable loss of his erection. In his job he frequently alternated between compulsive busywork—in a sense of being an industrious "father" to everyone in his office, giving plentiful advice, always being available—and a contrasting inertia and withdrawal from the work that was his precise professional responsibility. When particularly overextended, he would break down in exasperation and desperation that too much was asked of him. He feared he was unable to give a woman he loved what she wanted, feared that in general he was not masculine enough, that he lacked discipline in his work or sustained determination to see anything through to a clear conclusion. He longed then for the kind of unconditional loving he associated with his father, "that kind of benevolent love you want just to happen to you gratuitously and overwhelmingly."

As with Simon S. the main direction of therapy with Tom W. was to forge connections between the patient's conscious confusion and his unconscious feelings of panic and anger when he judged himself inadequate to a given situation, between his wish to be a father without having fulfilled his need to be a son, between his love for his father and his anger at his father's desertion.

The Wounded Archetype

Although Simon S. and Tom W. were very different people with different cultural, economic, and educational backgrounds, they both suffered a similar wounding in relation to their fathers. Both illustrate the kinds of problems a male may have when his psyche is cut off from its paternal roots, in whatever form. They also illustrate how a natural healing process is set in motion once they find reconnection to the father archetype. In these cases, such reconnection was not effected through the transference of the father role to me nor by way of conferring on me a mothering function. Rather, to use Jung's terminology, I seemed to embody the connecting function of their own psychologies, the anima that connects a man's ego to the deeper regions of his unconscious. Let me illustrate.

Both Simon and Tom felt only "half-formed." Simon depicted this feeling in his split body-images and fantasies of half-dead birds. Tom felt "dumb," unconscious where he should have been conscious. Thus both suffered a drastic abridgement of the begetting function of the father archetype, which they experienced sexually as fear of loss of virility, actual impotence, or confused sexual identity. They experienced that abridgment generally as a failure to sustain involvement with otherness—in Simon's case with another person, in Tom's case with his work. They both felt their egos as weak, without secure masculine identity, and deeply feared the strong pull of the unconscious. Simon feared he would be engulfed in his own pain if he allowed himself to feel. Tom feared he would sink more profoundly into the pervasive sleepy confusion he knew so well.

Both Simon and Tom tried to be fathers at an early age, when still in fact boys and sons, as if to protect themselves from the terrible loss of their fathers. Both grew up to enter fatherly professions, where others came to them to learn, to get comfort and advice. Both felt their work threatened by the unsatisfied longing to be a son. Hence they both became rigid and compulsive father figures, stuck in their roles without promise of renewal.

The two men felt weighed down by responsibility and inwardly impoverished, as if there was no one to offer nourishment to them. Turning to women availed little, and their sexual difficulties soon arose, because what they needed was sure connection to a generative source of meaning and order that would support their own ego development and not a mere sexual acting-out. Both men needed a conscious connection to the transforming dynamism of the masculine, symbolically depicted as the renewal of the father through the son, that is, renewal of the more developed ego parts of his psyche (the "father") by fresh new contents (the "son") always coming from the unconscious. Lacking the connection, both men alternated between playing the exhausting roles of father figures for others, giving away more than they had to give, and the equally enervating part of rebellious sons who defied those in authority over them without receiving any nourishment from them in return. Simon frequently felt trapped by rules and regulations, against which he vented his anger. He said at those times he "was flying high, free! No one could touch me!" Tom often sabotaged his own work by not giving reports on it to his superiors, simply ignoring their requests, whatever they were. Each man was riveted to his identification, as either the father or son aspect of the father archetype, with little sense of the fact that these were simply two sides of the same reality and either of them could become the means for the experience of self-renewal.

Instead of their strong emotions recharging them or pointing the way to new patterns of behavior, each man felt his aggression and his sexuality split off from the rest of him, with no hope of renewing the structures within which he lived. Each felt threatened. Each thought he had to choose between an ordered existence that was half-dead or a tumultuous and chaotic one. Simon, for example, at times succumbed to instinctual orgies of one kind or another— eating great quantities of highly seasoned food, dancing wildly far into the night, or engaging in sexual tempests with little or no sustained relationship to his partners. When let loose, his anger took giddy unrelated turns, poking sadistic fun at his adversary, leading him into manic expenditures of energy as if he never had to come down to earth again. Tom would let himself go in periods of inertia and messiness. His aggression would find a passive route to its target, either masking his omnipotence in a desire to help everyone or forcing him or the other person to hold on tenaciously even though he had registered signals that the best thing to do was to flee the situation. In both cases, the sex or aggression did not lead back into the center of their lives but rather moved away from it, reenforcing the feeling of ego weakness and of being undermined by forces from below. As a result, each man came to distrust the unconscious. They had little connection to the comforting aspect of the masculine spirit that conveys the unit of instinct-backed emotions and life's order and meaning. They both had lost hope of ever achieving a deep accommodation of consciousness to the unconscious and felt themselves therefore unconnected and unsupported.

Inwardly Simon and Tom suffered a gap where there should have been a connection between consciousness and the unconscious, just as they had suffered the great gap left by their departing fathers. The forces of their unconscious feeling lives—of sex and aggression—had not achieved sufficient humanization but had simply burst out in

episodes, then receded out of reach of their egos. Because
each felt his mother to be more rejecting than nurturing, to
each the maternal birth-giving aspects of the unconscious
seemed very far away from conscious use. Each man held at
bay a large store of repressed material. Simon, who
consciously felt rejected by his father and angry at him, had
repressed what love he and his parent had shared. Mixed
with his pain at having lost his father was the love he felt he
and his father had shared but not openly expressed. Tom,
who retained memories of an open love for his father,
needed to face and to feel consciously his strong outrage, the
anger that his father could have left him and not asked to see
him again until he was actually dying.

It was at the point of making these connections that each
man's work in therapy found its strength and clarity. My
principal role in each case was as an agent of connection to
the unconscious. Neither man related to me as if I myself
were a parent figure nor was either transference dominated
by sexual feelings. Unlike a maternal surrogate who would
be identified to her patient for a time as the unconscious, I
seemed rather to be experienced by each man as a receptive
and focused awareness of the unconscious. For quite a while
I carried this function for each man in our work together.
Then gradually each man took it over for himself. Simon
began to let himself consciously feel pent-up pain that he had
repressed. He began to see how he could use his fine rational
powers to be compassionate and eventually to understand
his father's point of view. Increasingly he felt that his reason
could live alongside his feelings, each stimulating the other.
In allowing himself to feel this pain, Simon began to feel as
well the pent-up caring he had in general withheld from life.
He felt lighter, happier, on the way to risking more feeling
involvement with others. Tom became more aggressive in
our sessions, trying to shape their focus and outcome in a

direction he chose. In the group he relinquished his overeager concern with others and concentrated upon what he wanted to get for himself. This act of connecting to himself brought him into authentic contact with the rest of the group members in much the same way as he had begun to connect his outer and inner selves, his conscious and unconscious lives.

Tom traced the source of his anger to his own unconsciousness, indeed to the fact of the unconscious existing at all. He had always felt he should not be unconscious; he should know the things he did not know. What came to light was not Tom's unwillingness to accept limitations, but rather his angry disappointment that his father had not been there as he grew up to instruct him in things, to teach him how to live. His father should have been there; he could not accept the fact that there were things he did not know because his father did not teach them to him. It was not, he finally realized, the unconscious that should not exist; it was the absence of his father that should not have been allowed.

Both Simon and Tom, then, in the course of their therapy effected reconnection to lost paternal roots. After initial periods of mistrust toward me and the split-off unconscious I symbolized, each began to make the painful descent of the dead, the confused, and the trapped areas of their own psyches. As indicated above, the primary role unconsciously entrusted to me by both men was that of a responsive, present, alert, reacting, personal connecting link to the repressed traumas and cut-off areas of a functioning life held fast in the unconscious. Each man gradually took back to himself this present, alert, and caring attitude toward his own psyche, thus bringing the split-off contents into direct relation to his ego-consciousness. The growth of their egos allowed them to be fed from the unconscious with the things they needed, such as emotion, focus, and some guidance for the future. Moreover, each man now needed less energy to enforce repression and hence had more energy available to him to be released into relationship and work. Reforging connection to the unconscious restored their hope in life and renewed in them a sense of life's possibilities.

Both Simon and Tom had had to develop too early a man-sized kind of male responsibility, or at least thought they had. Now they had the beginnings of psychic maturity and some of the connections that came with it. They began to grow roots downward. They felt more grounded in being; their confidence in themselves increased. They felt something like sureness, each of them. Simon chose to embark on another journey across the sea to try to see if his roots were there in his second homeland in Europe. Tom came to understand his former rejection of the unconscious and now willingly allowed himself to connect to it in periods of dreamy imagination and meditation. His confidence grew with his ability to make connections in his own way and with his own authority to his work, to the people he loved, to the meaning he found in life. His dreams reflected a buoyant sense of renewed life in such humorous examples as the following dream. In it different aspects of longing and aggressive self-assertion are united in the same psychic reality; a down-to-earth humanity is linked up to cosmic aspiration.

> I was talking to D., who is a big strong Bronx kid with a warm personality and soft heart. He was saying either, "I want to be a major," or "I want to be in charge," or "I want to be a bear." I said to him, "You are big enough to be Ursa Major—that's the big bear in the sky—that would make you Major Bear."

The experience of both these men led to the heartening and surprising discovery that when the connecting links to their own paternal roots were reestablished, the inner psychic momentum of the father archetype was again set in motion. The missing father was, they saw, to be found within them. Something interrupted and disconnected was once more joined. This restoration of the father archetype at the center of their lives helped guide each man toward better inner response toward outer situations and strengthened masculine identity. Each man felt more confident of being able to make a use of basic life situations that could nurture him and make him grow comfortably within such situations, thus connecting to other persons in a much more vigorous way.

Conclusion

These two cases illustrate a major Jungian conviction: The strength of fathering patterns lies in being open to the ways of bringing together inner and outer life that are distinctively masculine. The full significance of this conviction or perception, based on examples such as these, is still, I think, to be fully grasped. For the present it may be necessary simply to record one analytical experience after another in the exploration of archetypes, so that we can develop that familiarity without which any serious grasp of fathering in the sphere of depth psychology will be impossible. The world of the father has obscure and subtle dimensions that escape easy verbalization. That should not keep us from working attentively and meditatively with its mysteries.

Chapter IV

The Absent Father

William M. Lamers, Jr.

Yet can I not but mourn because he died
That was my father, should have been my guide.

Hartley Coleridge

The nature of the father–child relationship has been discussed elsewhere in this book. The phenomenon of the absent father has received relatively scant attention in the sociological and psychological literature despite the fact that through study of the impact of the absent father, a good deal can be learned about the essential nature of the father–child relationship.

Several factors play a key role in determining the impact of the loss of the father or the absence of father upon the developing child. They are:

1. The age of the child,
2. The presence of a replacement for the absent father including father substitutes, father surrogates, siblings, and extended family,
3. The nature of the father–child relationship,
4. The impact of absence of the father on the mother,
5. The timing of the disruption of the father–child relationship.

In theory, the above factors can be delineated and discussed as separate entities: in practice, the father–child relationship is extremely complex. And the impact of the absent father on the child is multidimensional rather than unidimensional.

The Age of the Child

The reaction of children to loss of one or both parents varies with age. The studies of Bowlby,[1] Spitz,[2] Freud,[3] and others outline the variables involved for children of different ages. The recent work of Holmes lends weight to the premise that loss of family members has significant impact on those remaining although that impact may not be obvious in physical or behavioral changes for several years.[4]

If the father is absent prior to birth of the child because of death, divorce, separation, or placement of the child for adoption, the mother (or the adoptive parents) has several options for dealing with questions the child may raise in the future regarding the biologic father. If a surrogate father is available at time of birth or in early infancy they may choose not to tell the child at all or until some future date of the absence of the biologic father and the reason for that absence. This possibility also pertains in cases in which the child has been conceived by artificial insemination.

If the child is born into a family in which there are older siblings who had established a relationship with the now absent father the developing child will learn of the biologic father from the older siblings, whether or not a surrogate father is present.

The relationship of increasing age in childhood to the ability to understand and react to loss is an extremely important one that has been studied and reported at length, especially in the literature of the field of child psychiatry.[5] In brief, the infant relates most intensely with the mother as she is customarily the caring, nurturing figure in our traditions for the early stages of infancy in which the developing child requires almost continual care and has little ability to relate with persons verbally or to begin to explore the environment. With increasing age the infant learns to differentiate among those who hold him, care for him, and try to relate to him. With the passage of time the young child comes to learn of the similarities and differences between "mother" and "father." As physical and psychological attachments develop for parental figures, the inescapable anxieties that arise upon separation from one or both parents begin to make their appearance known in verbalizations and in behavior. Games like Peek-a-Boo and Hide-and-Seek no doubt owe their existence to shared separation anxiety on the part of both parent and child.

The developing child has difficulty conceptualizing absence or loss of parents and usually is unable to begin working through the absence or loss of one or both parents until he or she is assured that someone will continue to provide food and shelter and care. The young child also has limited experience in facing and dealing with loss compared to the older child or adult, and is thus hampered when faced with the loss of a parent.[6]

Also, the young child utilizes "magical thinking" to cope with a world that he does not fully understand and that he cannot presume to control through the limited power available to him. In reacting to absence or loss of parents the developing child may assume, on the basis of magical thinking, that:

"I am responsible for what happened,"

"For punishment, the same thing will happen to me" (*e.g.*, I will be taken away),

"The same thing will occur to me when I reach the same age at which this happened to my parent."

With increasing age, the magical thinking of childhood gives way to the more conventional thinking of adult life, in which loss of a parent or absence of the parent can be dealt with in a more direct manner. Also, as the child ages there is less need for the parent to care for the child in terms of providing nurturance and shelter. But the psychologic need for parenting continues and may even increase during later childhood and young adult life to the extent that the child deprived of the presence of the parent of the same or opposite sex on a temporary or permanent basis may develop aberrations in psychologic-behavioral growth.

Substitutes for the Father

Granting the presence of a capable mother and a fairly stable environment, the temporary absence of the father should not be a matter for great concern. Temporary absence of one or both parents may even be looked upon as necessary factors in the development of children once we come to understand the necessity each child has to see himself as capable of existing and relating to the world without the immediate presence of one or both parents. But absence of one or both parents without the presence of satisfactory substitutes can have harmful effects on the developing child.

The primacy of the mother in human infant nurturing has been well established. Primate studies, including the work of Harlow, have given us an ethologic view of some aspects of the mother–child relationship that can help to illuminate the importance of parental substitutes, siblings, and the peer group in compensating for temporary or permanent loss of one or both parents.[7]

Age of the child at which absence or loss of the father

occurs has been discussed above. If replacement of the lost or absent father is made too soon, the child will be deprived of the necessary work of reacting to the loss of the parent. Replacement at too remote a time may not be of significant value if the child has closed off the possibility of ever relating to a substitute father figure. Pathologic assumption of the fathering role by the mother was seen in one family in treatment in which the mother urged her sons to "grow up and become a man like your mother." Excessive idealization of the absent father can cause the child to feel inadequate by comparison or can lead the child into an unnecessary competitive striving with the idealized yet absent father in hopes that this will compensate for the loss of the father or, as will be seen in one of the later clinical examples, may lead to a hoped-for reunion with the absent father.

No matter how adequate the substitute for an absent father, the complicated nature of the mother–father–child relationship usually precludes a smooth transition from father to absent father to father substitute. The child may resent the available father substitute as less qualified than the natural father as a way of symbolically stating that grieving for the absent father has not yet been completed; or, perhaps, that the child's anger toward mother for "letting father go" has not been satisfactorily resolved. Nonetheless, substitutes for the absent father can be of value depending upon a number of factors including the worthfulness of the father substitute and the way in which this substitute compares and contrasts with the idealized relationship the child had with the natural father.[8]

The Nature of the Father–Child Relationship

If the relationship with the absent father had been an excellent one, the child will most likely react with appropriate grief to the disruption of that relationship and will carry with him a conceptualization of the father that will have positive impact during the remaining years of childhood and on into adult life. On the other hand, if the relationship with the absent father had been an unpleasant one the child may be free to develop a more productive relationship with a father substitute that might compensate for the inadequacies of the earlier relationship.[9] But, at least in clinical experience, a variant of the second form is more commonly seen in which the developing child feels that he or she was in some way wanting or inadequate or overly assertive and that this is why the natural father went away, and the developing child or young adult enters into successive relationships with men that are designed more to reproduce the initial traumatic separation with all its resultant trauma than they are to establish solid, productive, and meaningful relationships with substitute father figures. We must remember when discussing clinical experience that the clinician sees a distorted sample of the population that includes primarily those who, in this case, have been unable to make effective or long-lasting adjustments to the absence of the father. Those who successfully make this adjustment do not come seeking therapy.

Impact of Absent Father on the Mother

If the father–mother relationship had been satisfactory, disruption of that relationship, especially through death of the father, would have profound impact on the mother and indirect impact on the child in addition to the direct effects the child would suffer through loss of the father. If the father–mother relationship had not been a satisfactory one, the long-range impact of absence or loss of the father may be quite different. The mother may experience relief at being freed from the relationship to her former spouse and may experience a period of personal psychological growth that may have positive consequences for the now fatherless child. On the other hand, if the mother blames herself for the failure of the husband–wife relationship or is unable to survive emotionally, socially, and economically without the support of the absent father, no matter what the quality of the previous relationship, then it is possible for the long-range effects of her difficulties to influence the ultimate psychological well-being of the child. [10]

Once again, the problems are multifactorial, and it is not easy to weigh each of the factors separately. Each child is also unique; one will thrive on circumstances that may cause another to regress.

Timing of Father's Absence

There are some important variables to examine when considering the timing under which the father becomes absent. At one extreme we will include the "purely biologic" father who conceived the child but who absented himself or died before the birth of the child. [11] At the other extreme it is important to consider the father who was always, in some way, available to the child but who was absent in the eyes of the child in terms of rendering the kind of fathering behavior that the child wanted or needed. [12]

On another level we must consider the father who leaves totally and abruptly through death or other circumstance and who has no continuing contact with the child. The father who is divorced or separated from mother but who returns on occasion must also be considered. The father who is periodically absent for fixed periods of time because of profession or occupation represents another variety of absent father that produces special types of problems for children.[13]

The "purely biologic" father is usually replaced by a stepfather or other father substitute and the child may have few, if any, problems stemming from this disruption of the normal father–child relationship. The essence of successful fathering is behavioral and attitudinal, not biologic.

The "always present but ineffective" father may be difficult to define and difficult to identify but surely causes a great deal of distress in children who yearn for a quality and quantity of fathering that is unavailable to them.

The abrupt loss of father through death or other circumstances usually has profound immediate and variable long-range impact on the child, once again depending on a set of variables including many of those discussed in this chapter. Loss that has been anticipated may, to some extent, be successfully worked through before the loss has been complete. Unanticipated loss results in grieving that may be experienced and expressed immediately or that, for various reasons, may be delayed in its expression. Grief may even be completely suppressed under unusual circumstances.[14]

The "periodically absent" father presents special problems for the child, somewhat similar to those faced by the child suffering abrupt loss of the father but usually complicated by the recurrent nature of the separation and by the temporary nature of relations with father surrogates plus the contaminating effects this type of recurrent separation usually has on mothers and other family members.[15]

Reactions to Loss

To understand the ways in which children react to absence of the father it is necessary to understand the ways in which children react to loss. Bowlby, Spitz, Lindemann,[16] and others have given us a framework in which we can begin to understand the universal nature of reactions to loss and have described the work that must be done in reaction to loss so that future social and psychologic growth is possible. A simple diagram (see opposite) outlines the sequence of reactions to loss.[17]

Bowlby uses the terms "protest," "despair," and "detachment" for the three major phases of reaction to loss. Each phase has its own characteristic emotional reactions (shown on the inner part of the circle) as well as physical or behavioral reactions (shown on the outer part of the circle). There is no fixed period of time in which these reactions occur. Anticipated loss (*e.g.*, from death due to a chronic illness) may be resolved to a large extent before the physical loss occurs; unexpected loss (*e.g.*, death through accidental means) may not be resolved until long after the customary period of mourning. Recurrent absence of the father through necessary business or professional travel or assignment may have effect depending upon a number of factors, several of which have been outlined in detail by Crumley and Blumenthal for the military family.[18] Crumley and Blumenthal have outlined some of the more common reactions seen immediately after departure of the father from the home:

1. Rageful protests over desertion,
2. Denial of loss and maintenance of an intense fantasy relationship with the lost parent,
3. Persistent efforts at reunion and restitution,
4. Arousal of irrational guilt and need for punishment,
5. Exaggerated separation anxieties and fears of abandonment,
6. Splitting of ambivalence toward the lost parent with a redirection of the hostility toward self or another,
7. A strong sense of narcissistic injury,

RECOVERY →

LOSS

PROTEST →
- SHOCK
- CONFUSION
- DENIAL
- ANGER
- ANGER AT SELF
- LOWERED SELF-ESTEEM

DESPAIR
- AGONY
- GRIEF
- ANGUISH
- DEPRESSION

DETACHMENT ←
- APATHY
- INDIFFERENCE
- LOSS OF INTEREST
- DESIRE TO WITHDRAW & "GIVE UP"

CRYING
PAIN
WEAKNESS
NAUSEA
LOSS OF APPETITE
SLEEP DISTURBANCES
OTHER PHYSICAL CHANGES

CONTINUING PHYSICAL SYMPTOMS

SLOWED THINKING & ACTIONS

"URGE TO RECOVER" THAT WHICH WAS LOST

DECREASED SOCIALIZATION
NO NEW FRIENDSHIPS
"BLAND" EXPRESSION
ABSENT SPONTANEITY

8. Decrease of ego control following loss of ego and superego support,
9. Precipitation of a wide variety of ego-repressive symptoms.

Within certain limits, these are normal reactions and are to be suspected or anticipated when a father leaves home for a considerable period of time. The degree to which these reactions can and will be resolved depends again upon a multitude of other factors, some of which have been previously enumerated. Attachment and loss go hand in hand; there is no attachment without potential loss, no relationship without potential separation. All separation and loss brings with it inevitable personality disruption, some immediate or early, some delayed or latent. The long-range impact of change in family structure on emotional and physical well-being has been carefully analyzed in epidemiologic studies conducted both in this country and in Europe. The terms "series of recent events" (SREs) and "life-change units" (LCUs) will become more prevalent as more people begin to realize the implications of the studies begun in mid-1950s by Hilgard[19] on the California State Mental Hospital population and followed later by the studies of Holmes.[20]

Social Considerations

It is interesting to speculate on the differing impact the absent father may have had on comparable families of prior generations. In prior years the father seems to have been more of a "presence" than in sectors of the current generations. For the father was by turns pioneer and visible laborer and breadwinner; today's father may take a commuter bus to a job he does not like where he works for a large corporation to earn money for a family that has little tangible evidence of his adequacy, much less his necessity. Coupled with the changing or less rigid parenting and identity roles of the husband–wife, mother–father and varying importance as a procurer of income for the family in a setting where mother–wife also works part or full time, the role of the father may have changed to such an extent that in some families loss of the father may have quite a different impact than that which we routinely presume.

For example, I recently heard of a daughter who said seriously to her mother, "Why don't you and Daddy get divorced so that I can spend all day Saturdays with Daddy like Sharon does with her Daddy?" The child of divorce at times spends more time and may derive more satisfaction from this time than was true prior to the divorce or separation.

Loss or absence of the father in today's society is also mitigated by the tendency toward smaller families, the wider prevalence of insurance and social security benefits to help compensate for death of the father, the widespread availability of day-care centers, nursery schools, and other preschool experiences for young children, as well as by the gradual acceptance of this society of women as an equal part of the labor force. More women have completed secondary education and college than was true of their parents and grandparents. The single parent, therefore, is not the exception.

The measure of successful parenting in a home where father is absent depends largely on the ways in which the necessary roles and duties of the father can be successfully assumed by the mother and/or various others in the community including siblings, relatives, neighbors, friends, teachers, and other partial father surrogates.

An increase in delinquency has been noted in the children

who have lost a parent through death.[21] Gregory suggests that the identification model provided and the control normally exercised by the parent of the same sex are more crucial in preventing delinquency among boys and girls than any aspect of the relationship with the parent of the opposite sex.[22] Glueck and Glueck in an earlier study made comparisons between five hundred persistent juvenile delinquent and five hundred nondelinquent boys matched for age, intelligence, and other background factors. They noted an increase in delinquency in those boys deprived of one or both parents in each of their five categories of broken homes: sporadic separation of parents, permanent separation or divorce, death, absence from home for at least a year on account of criminalism or illness, and abandonment at birth. In his study of Minnesota schoolchildren, Gregory found the highest rates of delinquency among boys whose parents were separated or divorced and who were living with the mother only. Higher than average rates of delinquency were also noted among boys who were living with neither parent as well as among those who had lost a father by death.

Impact of Loss of Father on Daughters

Loss of the father through divorce or death has some specific effects on daughters that usually is not apparent until adolescence. In a recent study Mavin Hetherington measured girls' ability to relate to men, either male peers or adult males. Dr. Hetherington noted that daughters of widows and daughters of divorced women felt ill at ease with men, compared to a control group that came from intact families. The teenager who lost her father through divorce was likely to be "clumsily erotic" with men; the adolescent whose father had died was more likely to be shy with men. These reactions seemed to be unrelated to the quality of the mother–daughter relationship and independent of the mother's apparent attitude toward men.

Scope of the Problem

Of the fifty-four million families in the United States, over eight million are single-parent families.[23] Four out of five single-parent families are headed by women. Between 1965 and 1973 there was an 80 percent increase (397,000 to 713,000) in the number of families headed by single mothers alone. Court records show that in custody cases following divorce or dissolution, women are awarded the children in 90 percent of the cases.[24] Single parents in this country are raising almost nine million children. Almost seven million children are being raised in families in which there is no father present, whether by divorce or death.

As the divorce rate increases and the number of single-parent families increases we cannot help but wonder about the possible long-range impact of this change on the children of divorce. Certainly, in many families the loss of the father brings with it the problem of decreased income and the matter of uncertainty of continuing monetary and psychological support. Many single mothers must modify their budgets and supplement alimony and child support payments with outside work. Credit is more difficult to obtain and the anxiety generated in the mother by economic pressure and uncertainty may be directly or indirectly transmitted to the child.

Additionally, the child of the single-parent family may be sensitized to loss and may unduly fear or anticipate the loss of the mother. Or the child may attempt to deny father's absence through hopefulness that father will return, thus making it at times more difficult for mother to cope with the reality of her loss and making it potentially more difficult for the child to accept a potential father surrogate into the family circle.

These generalizations may not prove to be the case. Loss or absence of the father may prompt the child to assume more responsible attitudes at an earlier age; the dependency of childhood that may otherwise have been prolonged may yield to a new awareness of the interdependency of the remaining members of the family and prompt early maturity that might otherwise not have developed. Once again, the important factors to consider in each case include the age of the child, the nature of the family and potential replacements, the nature of the father–child relationship, the impact of the loss on the mother, and the timing of the disruption of the father–child relationship.

Clinical Examples

The author's interest in understanding the dynamics of loss stemmed from years of working with patients who were in the process of reacting to the loss of someone or something important to them. The references cited in the footnotes pointed the way toward an improved understanding of the universality of reactions to loss that has broad application for clinical practice. What follows is a very brief selection of cases intended to illustrate some of the material presented above.

The Multiple Mothers

Bruce was the oldest of three sons born to a financially successful middle-class family. At age seven he learned of his father's death by suicide and later learned of his father's bisexuality. Bruce was raised by a covey of women including his mother, grandmother, and a succession of housekeepers and maids. He developed a great fondness for a man from another country who occasionally visited the family home. On learning of this man's death, Bruce entered into a period of ten years of alcoholism in which he dropped out of college, was arrested several times, and was unable to seek employment. His probation officer, sensing psychologic roots to Bruce's problems, referred him for psychotherapy. After several abortive attempts to develop a working relationship with his therapist he managed to stop drinking, complete college, work through the hostility toward his mother, develop successful relationships with several women, and settle down to a comfortable and productive life. Alcohol apparently was used as a way to avoid feeling or perhaps to prolong grieving for the father surrogate as well as for the natural father.

The Overprotected Father

Ann was the youngest of three daughters born to a conservative and industrious family. While her father worked his way up the executive ladder, her mother raised the children and sheltered father from any problems she might have had with them. Father was absent repeatedly on worldwide business trips. He cut short the one family vacation her mother had planned so he could return to the office. When Ann was eighteen her parents learned to their amazement that she had been using psychedelic drugs since twelve and had been sexually active since thirteen years of age. Both parents had trouble responding to Ann's criticism of her father's life-style and mother's compliance. They agreed to let her into a precipitous marriage to a young man they barely knew.

The Guilt-Ridden Daugher

Ellen was one of the most perplexing heroin addicts we had seen. She underwent withdrawal several times, mainly it appears, to reduce the cost of her habit. She was firm in her refusal to look at the reasons underlying her persistent addiction. One night when seen in the intensive care unit of a local hospital following a near fatal overdose, she asked to talk about the source of her abuse of drugs. Her story went something like this: "I was an only child, spoiled by my father. I could get anything I wanted. When I was seven we traveled to a family reunion. Mother said we should stay at a motel; I wanted to go to the farm to be with all my cousins. I raised a fuss and my father agreed to drive me out there—over mother's protests. I didn't know it for several weeks, but my father was killed in an accident on his way back to the motel. Mother left me at the farm for a couple of weeks and we never talked about Daddy's death. I started on alcohol at twelve and later found that heroin was the only thing that could make me forget the whole thing."

The Daughter of Divorce

Denise's parents divorced when she was five, shortly after her older brother died of cancer. Mother remarried when Denise was a young adolescent and soon became concerned about her daughter's obvious interest in older men. Denise eventually became involved with several men the age of her father and ultimately had a confrontation with her natural father that had many sexual overtones. She was referred for psychotherapy where her natural tendency to relate to older men in a seductive manner could be examined in light of its origins and impact on her life. Resolution of the transference to older men brought with it a noticeable diminution of her level of anxiety and an ability to settle into an appropriate choice of career and a comfortable marriage.

Implications for Care

Absence of the father from the home because of death, divorce, or occupation, as well as effective distancing of the father who remains physically in the household, will no doubt continue to occur. And the impact of this loss of the fathering figure will continue to be a potential impediment to the children raised in such a family. We can help to minimize any potential negative impact of loss of the father if we can understand the dynamics of the ways in which children react to loss and if we look for ways in which we can foster growth and development in spite of the absence of the father. The child needs to know the facts about father's absence and should be told in a caring way by the person responsible for care of the child. The child needs assurance that he will continue to be cared for and then needs time to work through all aspects of the natural sequence of reaction to loss that might include denial, fear, anger, self-recriminations, hostility toward the remaining parent, regressive behavior, delinquency, provocative behavior (testing limits), ambivalence, magical thinking, and any other type of behavior that may serve to express the confusion and disruption of loss of the father or absence of father from the home. Reaction to loss is a normal and necessary part of human growth and development. If this reaction is thwarted, if communication and expressive behavior are rigidly discouraged or overly controlled or if massive denial is used to pretend that the loss did not occur, then quite predictably there will be trouble in the years ahead. If, on the other hand, the reality of the loss is acknowledged and those involved are given permission to express feelings and to verbalize all the thoughts and reactions that come to mind, then there is a fairly good chance that the necessary work of grieving and bereavement can begin. Loss and its successful resolution can then become an integral part of life and growth, and the development of subsequent close personal relationships can include the necessary realistic awareness that, as Lucretius said, "No single thing abides, but all things change."

The child faced with absence of the father is at a temporary disadvantage. Whether or not this can be turned to a potentially positive situation depends to a large extent upon the awareness of those who are in a position to offer care and support during the early phases of this loss. Care and support of the child is not enough. The mother and extended family must also be included in the treatment program. Most of all, we must help increase community awareness of the special needs of the family with an absent father.

Chapter V

Loss and Grief in Fathering

John L. Maes

> The king covered his face, and the king cried
> with a loud voice, "O my son Absalom, O
> Absalom, my son, my son!"
>
> II Samuel 19:4 RSV

It would not be advisable to invite a person to write a
chapter on loss and grief in fathering who had not had
the experience of losing a child. In this respect the editors
have chosen well. The loss of a child was sudden, real, and
recent. Nevertheless, while the recency and power of the loss
of a beloved child gives authenticity and heart to the writing,
it may threaten any desired objectivity and general application of its content. The natural pitfalls would be to
overpersonalize and emotionalize the writing retaining
power and genuineness or to overobjectify it, losing the
power of personal experience. In this chapter a conscious
compromise has been struck. I will share the experiences of
loss and grief through my own phenomenology and then try
to make sense of them in the light of certain aspects of
contemporary theory and research.

Barbara

We sat as silent as a stone,
We knew, though she'd not said a word,
That even the best of love must die,
And had been savagely undone
Were it not that Love upon the cry
Of a most ridiculous little bird
Tore from the clouds his marvellous moon.[1]

I was shaving when the call came, preoccupied. Things
had been going badly at the college. Enrollments had been
gradually slipping. Money for program development was
scarce. The faculty had unionized, reducing administrative
flexibility and building defenses around mediocre perfor-
mance. The faculty and president had been at one another's
throats for two years. The board had hired a consultant to
study the presidency. Rumors, charges, and countercharges
ran rampant. Trust had decayed. Polarization, secrecy, and
hostility increased. As academic dean I was always in the
middle, forced frequently to make ethical decisions between
unsavory alternatives. Finally, after three years of stress, I
had made a terminal settlement with the college that was
financially advantageous but emotionally depressing. Now
the pressure was off. I was trying to carry off my symbolic
role with dignity and fairness but with a sense of hollow-
ness. Intellectually I knew I had not failed. Emotionally I felt
that I had.

These thoughts and others ran through my mind as I went
through the morning ritual. Then I heard my wife's quiet
voice on the phone. There was an edge of panic, almost
horror, in her tone. I rushed to the kitchen.

"That was Ed. He said Barbara is in the hospital and
they're fighting for her life. He said to come as soon as we
can."

A hurried call to the president and then into the car for a two-hour drive. During the anxious minutes my wife and I reassured each other. Barbara was the most vital person we knew, thirty-one years old, beautiful, radiant, graceful, and intelligent. Barbara had too much to live for, three extraordinary, vital, and endearing little girls and a successful husband. Barbara was a lover of art and music, an inspiration to her friends, a gracious hostess, an affectionate daughter.

We could understand her husband's concern and panic. Surely he must have exaggerated the situation. We hurried into the hospital and inquired where we might find her. The head nurse of the emergency ward came quickly.

"Hasn't anyone spoken to you?"

I saw the fear in her eyes. I said, "Is our daughter dead?"

The nurse told us of the efforts made to save her. The vital signs were kept alive for an hour and a half but no blood could circulate. The postmortem revealed a pulmonary embolism originating most likely in the pelvic area, which was small enough to pass through the heart but much too large to go through the lungs.

From that moment through the memorial service I became the rock for the family. Fortunately our house was a second home for the children. We made the necessary arrangements and took the family home. But Barbara stayed behind forever.

It was not until I was writing the eulogy for the memorial service that the full force of grief hit me for the first time. I wrote these words:

"Our beautiful Barbara was born May 28, 1945, in Owosso, Michigan. She weighed seven pounds, four and three quarter ounces. Being round, well-formed, alert, and responsive, she was instantly loved by everyone she met. As a two-year-old she held court every Sunday after her father's sermons, using her impressive repertoire of nursery rhymes, endearing glances, and brilliant smiles to charm her audience. From the beginning until the day she died, Barbara was vivacious, responsive, involved with people, and very charming.

"The serious Barbara lived behind and through this flowing *joie de vie*. She cared for her husband, Edward, and her three lovely daughters, Kristin, seven, Nicole, seven, and Heather, six, with a competence and compassion admired by all who knew her. As wife, mother, hostess, and friend, warmth, graciousness, and seriousness of purpose made the lives of those around her warm with practical love.

"Barbara was an intelligent woman, concerned about the political and social affairs of the communities in which she lived. She was unusually well read, having a particular interest in biography and English literature. Her enduring love for classical music, whether played by herself or others, was profound.

"Barbara put her intelligence to work with compassion. She prepared herself with a master of arts degree in special education. Then she taught and tutored deaf, retarded, and illiterate children and adults with great effectiveness.

"But the deepest Barbara only we, her family, knew. The inner beauty, the loving sensitivity, the softness, fragrance, and warmth of her can never be forgotten. Her belief in God, her respect for all people, her firmness and compassion with those who knew her well are indelible parts of our lives. Her beautiful life shaped us around her in positive ways. We became kinder, more honest, and more gracious because of what she was.

"Today we celebrate the life of Barbara, lived to the brim—'pressed down, shaken together, running over'— enough joy and love and peace for all of us.

"Child of love, a wife of deepest relationship, a mother of unsurpassed skill and compassion, a mature and intelligent woman in every sense of that good word, your life so short and so complete, until later, Barbara dear, we salute you and celebrate your life."

I sat at my desk with these words completed and wept torrents of tears. There then began the loneliest three months of my life. My wife went to live with the family so that the children could stay in school. We were together weekends with the children. It was a period of work, reading, pacing, and midnight television watching. But most of all, it was a period of self-evaluation, value evaluation, life evaluation.

The struggles at the college fell into perspective as role-playing, ladder-climbing, politicking substitutes for things that matter most: love, friendship, constructive leisure, intellectual and spiritual growth, marriage, and family building. I moved back toward the center of my being to my primary commitments as a clergyman and psycho-therapist, deepening my own meaning by helping others.

The ideas shared in the remainder of this chapter were mainly discovered in the reading and quiet contemplation that followed Barbara's death. I believe that the "vital lie" of my life has at last been penetrated by Barbara's death and the subsequent passing of my dear father who was terminally ill at that time. Yet the human spirit is strong. I have chosen to deal with my existential anxiety by confronting and learning from the experiences of grief and loss as fully as possible.

We had a remarkable relationship with Barbara: open, confronting, loving, and continuous. She lit our lives with her presence. Now she has become the inspiration for our deeper growth and reawakened sensitivity to the goodness of life and the beauty of human relationships.

> There was a man whom Sorrow named his friend. . . .
> Then he sang softly nigh the pearly rim;
> But the sad dweller by the sea-ways lone

Changed all he sang to inarticulate moan
Among the wildering whirls, forgetting him.[2]

Dependent Variables in the Management of Grief
and the Avoidance of Depression

In emotional terms, the sudden loss of a beloved child is like having a sturdy tree grown deep into one's being ruthlessly torn free by a bulldozer. When a tree is torn loose, the stages of separation are obscured by the noise and chaos of the trauma, only the serrated roots and gaping hole remain. It is in retrospect and by reconstruction of events that one can recall the tearing of the tender tendrils, the ripping of the roots, and the severing of the tap root. Each separate root fights to cling to its native earth as an immutable force tears it loose from life. And when the tree has fallen, the damage seems irreversible. It is forever.

The rupture of relationships in the sudden death of a loved one has many corollaries. The force is immutable, the separation is traumatic, and the damage seems irreversible. Only in retrospect can one examine the breaking of cathexes, the threat to ego integrity, and the confusion in identity. These are initially masked by merciful shock.

What are the variables that determine the degree and intensity of the sense of loss, the depth and duration of the grief process, and the rapidity or delay of the recovery? In "Mourning and Melancholia," Freud has carefully traced the similarities and differences between the normal grief process and the abnormal melancholia that we now label reactive depression, or psychotic depression, depending upon nature of the pre-morbid personality, the magnitude of the precipitating loss, and the extensity and depth of the traumatic regression.[3]

In this chapter I have chosen to deal with the post-traumatic grief process and recovery under the following headings: intensity and nature of the cathexes; strength or weakness of the pre-traumatic ego; quality and adequacy of surrounding ego supplies; availability of substitute objects; the balance between repression, substitution, and working through; and the willingness and ability to confront the grief and loss.

When a tree is pushed or blown over, nature, given time, will go far in the healing process without any help at all. The fallen tree will gradually rot away. The hole will partially fill through settling and erosion. New shoots will spring forth either from the broken roots remaining or from new seedlings. The scene of the trauma will ultimately have new life and beauty. So in the case of human loss. The wound heals, life goes on, the void is filled with new life experiences. Nature can be depended upon. However, there are better ways to fill the hole, clear the residue, plant the seedlings, and nourish new life. So in the case of human loss and grief there are ways to strengthen the ego, work through the grief, establish compensating relationships, deepen positive values, and develop new hope and vitality; yes, even joy in living.

Intensity and Nature of the Cathexes

I have always found the psychoanalytic term *cathexis* of great value in the understanding of personality. Like many terms used in the early days of psychoanalysis (and late nineteenth-century psychology in general) it is a blending of ideas from physics, physiology, and psychology. This term, used by Freud as a central concept in "Mourning and Melancholia," was defined by Strachey as a "term used on the analogy of an electric charge, meaning concentration or accumulation of mental energy in some particular channel. Thus when we speak of the existence in someone of a libidinal cathexis of an object, or, more shortly, of an object cathexis, we mean that his libidinal energy is directed towards, or rather infused into, the presentation of that object."[4]

Cathexes first occur in human beings as mental and emotional energy directed toward and attached to the mental representations (memories, fantasies, etc.) of the mother. If Freud is correct in his surmises, the first thinking in the human being occurs as action energy turned into thought by fantasizing the gratifying object—mother—when she is not, in physical fact, available. These cathexes are vital to the development and maintenance of the ego of the child. As Sullivan has pointed out, an entire dynamism of connected cathexes (thoughts, feelings, memories) gets built around the mother, this central figure in early human life.[5] The unique quality of sensitivity between mother and child built upon the consistent physical intimacy forced by the dependency of the child and the caring responses of the mother he called "empathy" (from the Greek *en* and *pathios*, literally feeling into).[6] It is reasonable, therefore, that the most intense and elaborated cathexes are from the mother to the child and from the child to the mother. Slightly less intense are those experienced from father to child and child to father.

Since fathers spend so much less time with young children than do mothers, the father must construct his mental representations of the child from less continuous physical contact and more impressionistic and secondary sources of data. It is likely that this leads to more projection and wish fulfillment in the father's mental representations of the child than in the mother's. Since she has had the continuous physical and emotional contact with the child, she may be both more protective and more accepting. She may have a better sense of the child's physical strengths and limitations and a greater willingness to accept the child as he or she is. This may account for the mother's more accepting "being" orientation to the child. The father is more apt to have a "doing" orientation with greater conditionality on love and acceptance. He may project more of his incomplete wishes for himself on the child, seeing the child as an extension of his own achievement dynamism. In either case the loss of a child may be a severe blow to parental self-esteem. The father may experience failure for not having protected the child from death as an outside intrusive force. The mother may experience loss of self-esteem for not keeping the child well, since feeding, nourishment, and health in general are her domain.

In any case, it is likely that the mother and father will be grieving over different mental representations of the same child since the nature of the cathexes are different.

A sense of powerlessness and personal failure can be experienced by a father whether the loss of the child is sudden or gradual. I recently had a long fireside discussion with my friend Alex whose daughter Marcie had died in her twenty-first year after a lifelong battle with cystic fibrosis. Marcie was diagnosed as having the illness at the end of three months of life. Alex's story was a touching litany of parental concern, medications, hospitalizations, recessions, and onsets of the illness. All of this was culminated with a three-day vigil in the hospital. Two major feelings stood out as Alex recounted the final hours of Marcie's life. The first of these was the feeling of helplessness and rage that it created. The second was a sense of having let Marcie down because he had left the room for a moment during which absence

Marcie died. He said, "I wanted to see Marcie all the way through."

It was obvious as we talked that Alex had gone through some of the decathexis before her death, that his attachments to her had undergone extensive transformations. Because of the openness of his and Marcie's communication, the reality of death had been faced and future expectations were resolved. But the grief and sense of loss was still profound even though the cathexis had been partially transformed and some of the grief work was already done.

The quality of a father's relationship with his sons and daughters is apt to be quite different. Sons more often become the direct extensions of the father's ego. This can be seen at several stages in the life of the child, but most clearly in the first few ambulatory years and again in adolescence. Small sons are encouraged by their fathers to incorporate paternally determined role models through imitation, competition, and relationship. The results of these early ego projections by the father can be seen in the vocational struggles of late adolescent boys and young men. At this stage, fathers try mightily not to impose their ego projections on their sons in the form of wishes for them to join the family business, get a good education "since I never had a chance," become a member of a distinguished profession, or some other wish-fulfilling expectation. Fathers often succeed in the manifest communication but fail completely in the latent unconscious communication. Hence it is common for the college counselor to work with a vocationally confused student who states with great sincerity, "My father wants me to major in whatever pleases me," while struggling with guilt caused by his unconscious awareness of the unconscious paternal wish. This problem generally gets dealt with in one of the following ways: (1) the son rejects the parental wish and chooses his own course in a reactive isolating manner, (2) the son gives up the battle to be separate and accedes to the parental wish, sacrificing self-esteem for dependency, (3) the father and son negotiate a decathexis of the parental wish projection and remake their relationship on new ground, freeing the son to be himself. In such an instance a mini-death has taken place, loss and grief have been experienced, and life has begun again on a new basis. The unconscious may be, "My son, the child, is dead; long live my son, the man." Such experiences of letting go by fathers and releasing dependency by sons are tiny dress rehearsals for inescapable loss that will occur when one of them dies.

The cathexes from fathers to daughters are, I believe, of a somewhat different nature. Instead of being directive and competitive such as he might be with his sons, a father is more apt to be permissive and tender with his daughters, at least until puberty. The direction of his wish fulfillment may not be to vicariously extend his own ego but to have his emotional needs met. Girls learn early in life to provide affection and ego support to their fathers. They learn to exchange emotional caring for physical protection and material indulgence and comfort. While this implicit contract has biological and even sexual geneses, it is also part of the role pattern of western culture against which contemporary women are rebelling.

This pattern of response in daughters tends to be strengthened to a pathological degree if the mother is seen as rejecting, cold, or punitive toward the father. This is also true if the father is overly seductive in his emotional relationship with his daughters. Such patterns of interaction result in neurotic (usually hysterical) patterns in the daughters when they become adolescents. This kind of pathogenic interaction is bound to complicate the grief process if either of the two persons dies. Freud's famous case of Dora is an example.[7] On the father's side, both the undue dependency on the daughter for emotional approval and feelings of guilt over inappropriate relationships complicate the grief process.

It has been my lot to help work out appropriate decathexes and transformation of relationships for several such persons, both fathers and daughters. While these therapeutic endeavors involved the death of mental representations of the ambivalently loved parent or child, they could be done in the context of a living object.

The death of a child, especially if it occurs suddenly, forces decathexis without allowing for continuation of the relationship. Hence the loss is double. The real child is lost with all the pain and joy, fulfillment or disappointment of that relationship. But the ideal image of the child is also lost with all its wish-fulfilling promise. It is these mental representations that are most difficult to overcome since they are composed of elements of both the "real" child and the "ideal" child; since they are within oneself, it is not uncommon to discover, somewhat to one's surprise, that viewing the body of a dead child helps resolve grief rather than exacerbating it. It may also be helpful later to look at pictures or movies of the child. In the first place, such activities tend to rectify the loss of the child, beginning the necessary process of decathexis. It also helps one to deal with the difference between the mental representations of the child and the physical reality. These representations rather than the "reality" are the attachments that constitute the major focus of grief work.

Koffka made the proposition that it is the perceived world rather than the real world to which we all respond.[8] Rogers pointed out that our phenomenological world, the world of our experience, is the emotional referent for us.[9] Rogers further made the point that the real world and the phenomenological world tend to come together as psychotherapy progresses, greatly reducing tension about one's relationship with the world.[10] This is akin to the task of grief work where the reality of the loss must be accepted and the mental representations brought together with unavoidable reality.

I believe that the loss of a child is more bearable when the real child and the mental representations in the father are more similar. In such a case the mental representations are more grounded in the facts of the child's physical and mental abilities and the degree of wish-fulfilling projection on the father's part has been less. This should allow the grief process to be more orderly and healing.

The Pre-Terminal Ego and the Grief Process

At best grieving is a painful process. In his study of London widows, Parkes discovered that the course of grief is fairly orderly and consistent.[11] He traced this process as alarm, protest, crying, searching, mitigation, and gaining a new identity. He found anger and guilt to be natural elements of this process that were gradually resolved. If loss and grief are used by the sufferer for optimal growth, they result in what Imara called a "radical transformation of our lives."[12]

The intensity of the grief process was captured in psychodynamic terms by Freud who likened grief to the symptoms of melancholia.[13] These symptoms he saw as profoundly painful dejection, abrogation of interest in the outside world, loss of capacity to love, inhibition of all activity, lowering of self-regarding feelings to the extent of self-reproaches and revilings, and culmination in delusional expectations of punishment. He stated that grief and melancholia were essentially the same process except for the degree of fall in self-esteem.

All persons permanently deprived of a love object through death experience temporarily debilitating symptoms. This is certainly true in the death of a child. Some fathers seem to be able to experience their grief openly, talk it through with trusted friends and loved ones, and endure and live through the grief without serious distortion of reality testing abilities. I remember that in the months after Barbara died, my sleep patterns were disturbed. I lived with a sense of alarm. My ability to organize and complete work was impaired. My emotionality was more labile than usual, tears came easily. For the first time in my life I wondered if it was really worthwhile to keep on living. I wondered once or twice whether I might really "flip out." All of this I believe to have been within the range of normal grief. It was like a moderately severe neurotic episode but with a clear objective focus and, of course, more sadness.

The boundaries of grief are not always so secure. Mental health practitioners and hospital chaplains have long known that losses are frequent precipitants to severe neuroses and even psychoses. Case histories of hospitalized psychotic patients frequently contain a series of losses. Probably the most psychodynamically damaging losses are the loss of one or more parents during young childhood. Early losses of this nature can leave ego damage that makes later losses very difficult to endure.

The basic psychological adjustment prior to the death of a child is probably the most important single determinant in the effect of that loss. The pre-terminal ego adjustment is more important than such issues as the nature, cause, or suddenness of the death of the child or the age of the child at death. If traumatic separations and losses have previously occurred in the life of the father, it would be wise to seek professional help as soon as the impending death is known or, in the case of a sudden death, immediately after it happens.

Cameron has pointed out that in the case of neurotic depressions "the regression revives an infantile struggle between an abnormally dependent ego and an abnormally critical superego." [14]

The risk of severe depression with self-punitive and self-abnegative attitudes is much greater in the case of an already damaged ego. If the ego is extremely weak with many traumatic early experiences and marginal management of reality, the regression under pressure of the anxiety caused by the death of a child may be so great that a psychotic depression will occur. In this case the father will be markedly slowed down physically, irrationally and insistently self-punitive, and angered by any attempts to logically counter these negative self-images. Hospitalization will almost surely be necessary since reality contact is so impaired and suicidal notions are so often present.

Short of such severe melancholia, the depth, intensity, and duration of the grief reaction will be greatly affected by the strength and resources of the pre-terminal ego. Such factors as self-esteem, good logical processes, clear perceptions of support resources, and the ability to use them are evidences of a healthy ego at any time. During a period of grief such positive ego functions become critically important. They allow a bereaved father to regain control of his life and assist him in working through a new identity using the painful loss of a child as an opportunity for a "radical transformation in his life." [15]

Ego Supplies and Substitute Objects

If a father's ego strength is such that he can manage grief without falling into pathological melancholia, the most important variables in the appropriate mitigation of grief are available ego supplies and appropriate substitute love objects. An analysis of ego supplies can be derived from the answers to the following questions:

Is the wife living?

If so, is the relationship with the wife open and warm?

Is she strong enough to carry her share of the grief without overprotection?

Are there other children?

Does the father have strong friendships of his own?

What are the continuing sources of ego income such as satisfying work or hobbies?

Has the father learned to use good reading material as a resource for thinking through problems?

What professional resources exist such as growth groups, trained counselors, or psychotherapists?

When Barbara died so suddenly, her husband and my wife and I went together to pick up the children at school. We took them into the car and held all three little girls while their father told them plainly and lovingly that their mother was dead. He explained that she had had the very best medical attention, but she had died of a blood clot in the lung. He reminded them of her beautiful life and how much we all loved them and would take care of them. During those moments we all faced the finality of her death together and became, more than ever, a family. During the months that followed, the children prayed for Barbara, often wished her back, but were never once unclear that she was gone and what were the physical reasons for her death.

The support community for us as a family and for me as a father was enormous. At the memorial service our friend Landon spoke with such personal understanding of Barbara and all of us. The young pastoral counselors whom I had helped to their doctoral degrees in pastoral counseling over the years came en masse. The young director of the music department at the college where I was academic dean played "Jesu Joy of Man's Desiring" on the harpsichord as he has never played it before or since. The volume of beautiful letters will never be forgotten. Relatives came from all over the United States.

In the subsequent months, friends have come for weekends, phoned long distance periodically to "see how you are," and on and on. It is strange how much the love of God becomes reified in one's mind by the actions of caring human beings.

Most of all we took time to talk and be together. All other considerations became secondary to the integrity of the family and the needs of three motherless children. One cannot in this short space give advice to unseen readers who may be grieving the loss of a beloved child. But I know from experience that ego supplies are there in the persons of family, friends, colleagues, and professional clergy and counselors. Your own bereavement is the time to remember the words of Jesus: "Ask, and it shall be given you; seek, and ye shall find; knock, and it shall be opened unto you" (Luke 11:9).

In working with depressed or bereaved persons I always strive to help them regain control of their lives, often painfully, one segment at a time through a process of ego lending and mastery. They learn to lean on the therapist without surrendering their own identity, never in the interest of dependency but always in the interest of greater problem-solving mastery of their own lives. In my own bereavement I have followed this course unashamedly— leaning briefly on my wife, friends, and colleagues, always in the interest of personal growth and a greater self-understanding and mastery of my existential situation.

There is no substitute for a lost child. Each human being is a completely unique, precious, and irreplaceable child of God. But in any human separation experience, all of which are little deaths, replacement of loss with new love objects is an effective part of reworking one's identity. One of the most dramatic examples I have known involved my friend Charlie. Charlie and his wife had never had children, though they longed for them. Finally when they were in their forties, a little son was born. The rejoicing, pride, and sense of fulfillment can hardly be described. But when the little son was two years old he became ill. The doctors diagnosed a fast growing carcinoma. The little child died of the cancer when he was only two and one-half years old. Charlie alone could speak of the depths of his bereavement and depression. He is a distinguished psychotherapist himself and entered psychotherapy. After he mastered the worst of his grief, he and his wife adopted a baby and rebuilt their lives and their home. I will never forget Charlie's courage. When Barbara died I found myself longing to have a child. But there was no reasonable way that a man and his wife in their early fifites should burden a child with their child hunger, especially since the full course of child rearing could not be guaranteed. We were also wise enough to know that we could not transpose our grandchildren into our children. But we can love and support them and their father. Perhaps a more effective substitution for me has been my decision to absorb the literature of grief, loss, death, and bereavement counseling so that I can effectively offer this service to other fathers, mothers, and children who are grieving. While the cathexes can never be the same as they were toward Barbara, these sublimations can, if well done, be doubly life saving—for me and for my clients.

Repression and Working Through

The economy of the human system is amazing in its arrangements for human survival. The state of shock following the death of a loved one allows one to function in a numbed, slightly dissociated manner to get through the first few days. It is later that the well of one's being is opened to allow sharp fragments of painful memory to escape into awareness. While massive repression of feeling is a feature of certain pathological illnesses such as severe depressions and catatonia and while chronic repression is the enemy of problem solving in neurotic personalities, the temporary repression experienced in grief is a lifesaver. But continued repression rigidifies the personality and obstructs the positive progress of grief. The secret of successful bereavement is the balance between repression and working through the grief. This involves the recovery of memories, the detachment of cathexes, deepening of self-understanding, and making a new life plan.

As can be seen in cases where the depression takes the form of mania—where emotions, thoughts, and memories are spilled forth without restraint—simply spilling is not very helpful. Compulsive discussion that runs ahead of feeling does not solve problems. In working through, feelings and ideation are brought together with the reality aspects of life. How does one feel and why? What can be done to make life more bearable? Who are the friends or professionals who can provide the warmth and objectivity needed to allow effective working through? Each father must answer these questions for himself. But whether it be one's wife, friends, minister, or professional counselors, there are likely some persons in one's environment who can be effective catalysts for this necessary process. Especially helpful might be a group of bereaved persons who can share the grief and renewal process together. At best it will take time, for grief has its own schedule for each person and should neither be delayed nor hurried.

Values Learned from Death

In discussing dying as the last stage of growth, Imara pointed out that one's own death is an opportunity for "original experience." [16] He said: "Our inner conflicts, our chronic guilts, our boredom and lassitude, and our acute loneliness begin with our denial of our own original creative experiencing."

He suggested that the dying person ask three questions: Who am I? Who am I in relationship? In what way will I live my life? He outlined five stages in coming to terms with one's own death: denial, anger, bargaining, preparatory depression, and acceptance. [17] There is little in his writings that I do not find true for myself as I experience the loss of my child. Any major disruption of routine is an opportunity to evaluate life with a new intensity and clarity. The loss of a child second only to one's own death has the power to penetrate what Becker called the "vital lie" of life. [18] Becker defined this term as "a necessary and basic dishonesty about oneself and one's whole life situation."

> All of us are driven to be supported in a self-forgetful way, ignorant of what energies we really draw on, of the kind of lie we have fashioned in order to live securely and serenely. Augustine was a master analyst of this as were Kierkegaard, Scheler, and Tillich in our day. They saw that man could strut and boast all he wanted, but that he really drew his "courage to be" from a god, a string of sexual conquests, a Big Brother, a flag, the proletariat, and the fetish of money and the size of a bank balance.

There it is. The greatest value of Barbara's death for me as her father was the stripping away of the "vital lie." The lie of role importance as a substitute for personhood, the lie of elaborate theological rationalizations as a defense against my need for God and my helplessness before him. There came to me afresh things that I had dimly known to be true—the importance of rest, beauty, and health. I work at home now in my study-office, reading, writing, training therapists, doing psychotherapy, cutting wood, looking out the windows at the mountains. Now I know I will never be as great as I was driven to be but better perhaps than I thought I could be.

Thank God for Barbara's legacy—the warmth of children, a new look at life, a closer family, the penetration of the "vital lie," and all the beautiful memories of Barbara flashing by, cooking, bending, smiling, lifting children, playing the piano, arguing with flashing eyes. She left her father rich indeed. Winifred Welle's poem "Climb" might have been written just for her, as if she had spoken the verses:

> The timid folk beseech me, the wise ones warn me,
>   They say I shall never grow to stand so high;
> But I climb among the hills of cloud and follow vanished
>   lightning,
>   I shall stand knee-deep in thunder with my head against
>   the sky.
>
> Tiptoe, at last, upon a pinnacle of sunset,
>   I shall greet the death-like evening with laughter from
>   afar;
> Nor tremble in the darkness nor shun the windy midnight,
>   For by the evening I shall be a star.

Chapter VI

Refathering in Counseling and Psychotherapy

William A. Kelly

Introduction

As a father I am committed to good counseling, when it is appropriate, with my children. And as a counselor-psychotherapist I am committed to good fathering, when appropriate, with the people who contract with me for my professional service.

In western society in the twentieth century, fathering has been a neglected vocation. The absence of the father has been a major theme of many recent studies of the family in evolution.[1] Popular books on parenting have tended not to distinguish between what fathers do and what mothers do in influencing the development of their children or else they have been written primarily with the assumption that it is the child's mother who carries the burden of parenting in the family. Until recently, that is. For now—in the 1970s—books, magazines, and daily newspapers have reflected a new concern about, appreciation of, and instructional information for men who take their paternal tasks seriously. Writing for parents, Henry Biller and Dennis Meredith have affirmed: "Father power is different from mother power, and your child needs both in order to develop properly."[2]

Social scientists interested in children—sociologists, psychologists, physicians, educators, psychotherapists—have made a major contribution to parents who are ready to learn more and to approach their relationships with their children in deliberate, informed ways. In the field of professional psychotherapy, there has also been taking place within the past decade a renewed interest in the possibilities of intentional reparenting within treatment and educational settings. While our understanding of the elements of good parenting and good psychotherapy is still limited, it is nonetheless true that we have accumulated valuable knowledge about these patterns of complex human interaction.

I see a growing consensus about the qualities and functions of a proficient parent and an effective professional helper, an agreement based on what we have learned about the dynamics of healthful interpersonal relationships and about the orderly changes through which persons progress, in the course of a lifetime, from infancy toward bio-psychosocial maturity.

In *Father Power*, Biller and Meredith pursue the idea of "social fatherhood . . . the feeling by adult family men (the 'establishment' in a positive sense) that they have a responsibility to see to society's proper functioning."[3]

> In growing into fatherhood, a man learns the true meaning of nurturance and gains a confidence that he can have a deep effect on others—adults as well as children. After gaining this confidence and the necessary skills from interacting with his children the adult male tends to apply them to his dealings with his environment, his neighborhood, his city, his nation, and his world.[4]

This chapter is an exploration of the possible meaning of social fatherhood in a particular extrafamilial relationship, that of the man who is a counselor or therapist with those who come to him for help. I see the issues and principles that arise out of this discussion as relevant not only to specialized practitioners of psychotherapy but to the broad range of those who are socially identified as "helpers," to doctors, lawyers, clergy, teachers, social workers, and the many others whose professional business is attending to the education and well-being of people. The discussion is of concern to women as well as men. Not only in their families, but in the world of work, many women and men exercise profound parental authority and perform extensive parental functions for their constituents, customers, clients, patients, subordinates, or co-workers. It is my conviction that our society needs in every sphere of living—in the realms of play and of politics, commerce and education, religion and industry—not *less* parenting but *better* parenting, good fathering *and* good mothering, parenting through which people are led beyond the unsureness, wishfulness, and dependency of childhood into the personal autonomy, self-confidence, and social usefulness for which we all have potentiality.

Three Experiences in Psychotherapeutic Fatherhood

In this portion of my essay, I want to present three case illustrations, from quite different sources, to throw into relief the theme of refathering in psychotherapy. The materials on "Mrs. K.," "Dennis," and "Nancy" demonstrate how occasions for refathering may arise and indicate some of the ways therapists have learned to respond.

Mrs. K.

In his book *The Technique and Practice of Psychoanalysis,* Ralph R. Greenson observed, "I believe the ideal analyst is a motherly father figure or fatherly mother." [5]

One patient history he reports is that of "Mrs. K." At the time she came for treatment with Dr. Greenson, Mrs. K. was twenty-seven years old. She had been married to an older man for two years and was the mother of an infant daughter. Mrs. K. had been the oldest of her mother's three children. Her father had deserted the wife and child when the patient was one and a half years old. Her mother went through three additional marriages, and as a child, Mrs. K. had experienced poverty and family disorder. She came for help because she was bothered by persistent sexual fantasies and impulses toward promiscuity. Greenson traces out the ways in which Mrs. K. came to react to him as if he were her parent. Mrs. K. responded to the analyst with a sense of shame, as if he were not only her strict father but also her compulsively clean mother of toilet-training days. Gradually she realized that the analyst was not afraid of her impulses or repelled by her aggressive fantasies and that he was determined to continue the work with her, so that he became a "father protector."

> She was torn, on the one hand, by her desire to be a good patient and reveal all her weaknesses, and, on the other hand, by her wish to be loved by me, to be found sexually and mentally attractive, and therefore to hide her defects. I was to make restitution for her lack of a father by making her my favorite patient and by doing for her what I would not do for any of my other patients. I would be the ideal, incorruptible father of whom she would be proud and also the delinquent father who would satisfy her incestuous wishes. Very early Mrs. K.'s symptom of promiscuity impulses shifted to me, as an oedipal figure. This alternated with an image of me as the stern, disapproving, and puritanical, idealized father.
>
> As she trusted me more she also dared to feel some primitive hatred and rage toward me. . . . She could also love me as her good investment, her security for the future, her guarantee against emptiness, the man who gave her substance.[6]

In the course of her psychoanalysis, Mrs. K. began to find greater pleasure in heterosexual relations and in her family relationship with her daughter. She became less fearful of childhood feelings toward her mother and eventually was also able to express violent feelings of hatred toward the analyst as a male.

> When the patient was able to express these feelings and find that I was neither destroyed nor antagonized she began to feel that I loved her and accepted her unconditionally and permanently . . . even when I did not agree with her.[7]

Mrs. K.'s analysis lasted for four and one-half years. Dr. Greenson's notes allow us to follow the path along which, through the experience of a consistently dependable and regular relationship with a man who listened with compassion to her, accepted whatever she had to say, searched for and shared with her insight into the meanings of her thoughts, Mrs. K. moved toward greater self-acceptance and more satisfying adult relationships. We catch a glimpse of the intense way in which she focused on the analyst her symptoms, conflicts, impulses, wishes, and defenses. Greenson does not report his own personal reactions; he does suggest the value of his patience, presence, and concern combined with a certain detachment. A sense of personal warmth, commitment, and humaneness pervades his writing.

While Greenson does not use the term "refathering," we discern how he became indeed a "motherly father figure or fatherly mother" for this woman who had been deprived of fathering and subjected to inconsistent mothering.

Dennis

The person primarily responsible for introducing the concept of reparenting into prominent usage in the field of psychotherapy has been Jacqui Lee Schiff. A clinical social worker trained in transactional analysis, Jacqui Schiff came to believe that, contrary to prevailing psychiatric opinion, seriously dysfunctional persons could undergo major personality change if in place of the defective parenting of their early childhood they were provided with a comprehensive experience of thorough, consistent, nurturant parenting, that is, if they were given a "second chance to grow up." She and her husband, Moe, developed their method of reparenting in response to the needs of teen-agers and young adults who had been diagnosed as severely schizophrenic. Their basic approach was to take these disturbed "children" into their home and treat them in the same way they cared for their own three natural sons.

Jacqui Schiff has recounted the decision she and Moe made to accept Dennis, a boy in his late teens, into their home.

> A child needs, above all else, a mother. He must be held and stroked, fed and bathed, and loved. He needs a healthy family with two responsible parents. . . . What I was proposing to attempt with Dennis involved a total rebuilding of his personality, exposing his Child to an entirely new parental and societal experience, on the assumption that he would then have a choice between a pathological and healthier personality structure.[8]

Jacqui Schiff's report includes a reconstruction of Dennis's own inner response:

> She doesn't frighten me. She could be my mother. I wish she'd be my mother. I've been searching for a mother since I was thirteen. But when she knows how bad I am, she won't want me.[9]

The book *All My Children* is the account of the Schiffs' experiences as parents to Dennis and several other boys and girls whom they sought to "bring up" to social maturity through good reparenting. Dennis· became a permanent family member, received a new name, and eventually became a professional therapist himself, collaborating with his "mother" in her work.

Among the distinctive features of the work of the Schiffs are their commitment to providing their children with a total, twenty-four-hour-a-day new life in a family; their willingness for the children to regress into the dependencies of infancy and early childhood and to care for them precisely at that regressed age-level; and their use of their own natural propensities for good parenting. She has described her husband and his increasing involvement as father to the new children.

> Moe is instinctively attracted to all children who need fathering . . . a marvelous, natural father: committed, intelligent, and infinitely loving . . . an outspoken, outgoing, genuinely emotional man.[10]

On one occasion Moe, in disciplining one of the boys, made a mistake and hit the boy unjustly. When Moe sat blaming himself harshly, another boy came up to him and said,

> "But, Daddy, if you don't do it, who else is going to do it? You're the father and you have the right. There's no one else. You're the end of the line." Moe stared at Mark for a long moment, and then, as he said later, "everything suddenly fell into focus. I realized that if this boy—or any of the others—was going to get well I was going to have to love him like a father loves his own son—and whack him when I thought he needed it, and hug him when I felt like it. Otherwise, he would never make it. And if he, and the other kids, were willing to believe I was their father and had a father's rights, then who was I to argue? If they believed in me and I believed in them, and I happened to guess wrong once in a while, we'd all still survive."

"That," Jacqui Schiff comments, "was the turning point for him, the moment he changed from being a 'social worker playing father' into a full-time father."[11]

Nancy

When, during a therapy session, a client makes a shift in consciousness from present-oriented thoughts and feelings to a set of sensations, emotions, and thoughts that are like those he or she experienced at an earlier age, the phenomenon is called "regression." What is striking about the regression shift is that the person does not simply remember and think about an event out of his or her past but actually senses, feels, and sometimes acts as if he or she were completely "back there" in that earlier time. Most people experience moments of regression, a return to childlike reactions, occasionally. Stress is a frequent triggering cause of regressed awareness. In psychotherapy, regression may occur spontaneously, or it may be induced deliberately by the way a therapist and client work together. Frequently, the regression shift provides new information about the client's earlier experience and may open up the opportunity for resolving an inner conflict or working a behavior change.

Freud's earliest use of hypnosis in treatment involved first regressing the patient back to a traumatic moment in infancy or childhood, then assisting the patient to abreact, *i.e.*, to express directly and openly in the treatment setting the strong feelings which had been aroused in that earlier event but had not been given an outlet. Jacqui Schiff's reparenting of disturbed patients also makes use of regression. In a safe setting the "children" are allowed to experience old feelings and needs, then are provided with whatever attention and assistance might be necessary to enable them to develop and adapt to their present world in healthy ways. Many psychotherapists today use temporary, brief regressive episodes to enable a patient or client to make specific changes in the direction of greater personal freedom, satisfaction, and effectiveness. One of these is transactional analysis therapist Russell E. Osnes who has given a report on what he has called "spot reparenting" in a group counseling setting.[12] His intention is to reconstruct a part of the Parent ego state and to correct the confusion of the Child ego state "by giving him an experience of nurturing and warm caring to replace the traumatic hurting which was experienced in the original parenting."

> My clients go back to an actual experience, relive it to the point of the negative parenting or some other crucial point in the negative experience. At that time I intervene with the Nurturing Parent, which was needed in the original experience.[13]

A special feature of spot reparenting is the way in which the therapist, using the clues of voice tone, language, body movement, and direction information that the client offers, seeks first to identify in a very specific way the age and situation into which the client has regressed and then to provide parental attention precisely appropriate to the child in such circumstances. If the person seems to be reliving an event from infancy or very early childhood, Osnes will allow volunteers from among the group members actively to provide nurturing for the regressed person, since "the infant doesn't know how to ask with words and the very young may have given up asking."[14] By the time children are older than two or three years of age, they are able to ask for what they want for themselves, and a client who cathects to an age beyond two is asking directly for the nurturing he or she needs.

Russell Osnes provides the illustration of his work with a woman named Nancy, who wanted to deal with her fear of authority people and especially her father.[15]

I asked her if she wished to become young again and see what answers could be given for her fear. She agreed. Our procedure went like this:
"Close your eyes, Nancy . . . what are you feeling?" "Afraid."
"OK, would you go in your fantasy to a quiet place all alone where it is totally safe and you have nothing to fear? You will not be frightened here."

When in her imagination, Nancy could find no place where she felt safe by herself, the therapist asked her if she wanted him to go along.

She said, "Yes." [Later Nancy said: "I felt safe because I wasn't going alone—I wouldn't get stuck back there, and I had your protection against getting beat."] I took her hand and she quickly cathected young.
"How old are you?"
"Five."
"Where are you?"
"Upstairs in my room with my sisters."
"What is happening?"
"They are trying to get me to hurry and get dressed because father has given us all just a few minutes to get downstairs. I'm dawdling, fantasizing that I'm a princess at a ball 'performing' for my sisters." ["It was worth a beating to be me, a princess, for a few minutes."]
"Then what happens?"
"They leave me and go downstairs."
"Now what's happening?"
"Father is at the bottom of the stairs and demanding that I come down this instant."
"Are you going?"
"Yes, I'm going down the stairs scared and trying hard to get my pajamas on while I am going down."
"OK, you're at the bottom of the stairs, now what happens?"

Father is hitting me, I'm scared, and crying . . ."
"Nancy, what do you need right now instead of what father is
doing to you?"
No answer. ["I did not dare to answer, if I talk I'll get hit
again."]
"Nancy, what do you need right now instead of what father is
doing to you?"
"I need to be loved instead of hit."
"Is there someone here that you would like to have hold you
right now?"
"Yes, George." [Her husband.] "Will you hold me?"
"She sat in George's lap, snuggled up warmly and was touched
and supported by others. "George rocked me—I have no other
memory of being rocked, it felt great."

As Nancy's husband held and rocked her and told her, "I
love you. You're a beautiful person," Russell Osnes, the
therapist, said to her, "You don't have to be afraid any more
Nancy, father isn't going to hurt you again. It's OK to get
your needs met, and to be loved."

These three illustrations—Ralph Greenson's long-term
work with Mrs. K. in psychoanalysis, the reparenting that
the Schiffs undertook with Dennis and other needing
schizophrenic "children," and the directive "spot reparenting" of Nancy reported by Russell Osnes—serve to introduce
certain common themes and issues in the discussion of the
fathering role of men who are counselors or
psychotherapists. In each instance the therapeutic work
included the provision for an atmosphere of safety, the
establishment of a setting and of communication rules that
facilitated change, and the dependable presence of a man
who acted with both assurance in himself and acceptance of
the other. In all three illustrations, the therapy was directed
toward a fuller measure of adult autonomy and satisfaction
for the client. In an interesting way all three of the patients
changed in the direction of more fulfilling family relation-

ships: Mrs. K. with her husband and daughter, Nancy with her husband in the group setting itself, and Dennis with the Schiff family. The three male therapists were called upon to provide more than informed, rational advice and instruction. To be effective, each had to communicate concern, empathy, support, and understanding without preventing the client-"child" from experiencing his or her own "growing pains."

For my purpose in this chapter, I shall use the term "refathering" broadly, to apply to all those interactions between therapist and client that have a father-and-child quality. I am writing in advocacy for a greater awareness, in all professional helper relationships between men and their clients, of the parent–child dynamics of those relationships. I am proposing that in psychotherapy we make bolder use of what we know about effective fathering. My intention in what follows is to open up certain basic issues, the discussion of which must, it seems to me, continue to inform any clinical practice of refathering—the dynamics of transference and counter-transference in the therapeutic interaction, the strong feminist reaction against the domination of the field of psychotherapy by father figures, and the influence of sexuality on the relationships between therapist-fathers and client-daughters. The final section of the paper is a reminder for all of us who participate in the healing, the learning, the unfolding, the maturing of others, that the process leads beyond parenting.

Transference Reconsidered

When at the early stages of this chapter's preparation, I told a friend that I was writing about fathering in psychotherapy, she replied, "But isn't that just the transference?"

Anyone who has studied psychology in the past forty years might be presumed to know about what Freud called "transference," the way in which a client displaces onto a therapist reactions that were originally directed toward the client's parents. Until fairly recently the theory and technique of psychoanalysis had dominated training programs in counseling and psychotherapy, so that attention to transference phenomena had been a basic consideration in carrying out any good therapy. Yet, with the reaction against the psychoanalytic approach to psychotherapy, transference reactions in the relationships between client and therapists or between trainees and teachers seem to have been given less scrutiny. Many a neophyte counselor has become embroiled with a client because he had not learned to recognize and counter the client's childlike pulls, resistances, and pressures. I remember well the comment a senior psychiatric social worker made to a group of us in counseling training a number of years ago to the effect that by neglecting transference dynamics in our earnest search for new, speedier methods for helping people, we were choosing not to use one of the most powerful tools for effecting change available to us. Out of my own experience in counseling and teaching, I have concluded that there is value in considering again what Freud learned and sought to teach those who came after him.

In one of his later writings Freud defined transference as the tendency of neurotics to

> develop toward their physician emotional relations, both of an affectionate and hostile character, which are not based upon the actual situation but are derived from their relations toward their parents. . . . Transference is a proof of the fact that adults have not overcome their former childish dependence; . . . it is only by learning to make use of it that the physician is enabled to induce the patient to overcome his internal resistance and do

away with his repressions. Thus psychoanalytic treatment acts as a second education of the adult, as a correction to his education as a child.[16]

The intense emotional relationship between patient and analyst "can be of a positive or a negative character and can vary between the extremes of a passionate, completely sensual love and the unbridled expression of an embittered defiance and hatred."[17]

It is possible to distinguish between an intense *transference relationship*, which is likely to develop between analyst and patient in the course of a long treatment across a broad range of attitudes, feelings, and wishes, such as was illustrated by the analytic work with Mrs. K., and *transference attitudes*, which may occur between any two people who are important to each other. Ralph Greenson has summarized the latter, broader meaning of the concept:

> Transference is a reliving of the past, a misunderstanding of the present in terms of the past.
> Transference occurs in analysis and outside of analysis, in neurotics, psychotics, and in healthy people. All human relations contain a mixture of realistic and transference reactions.[18]

Transference attitudes are probably a feature of every intimate relationship—between marriage partners and lovers, between close friends, between doctors and patients, priests and parishioners, charismatic leaders and their followers, teachers and close students. Mutual transference is one of the bonds of long-lasting companionship. Unconscious, unrecognized transference reactions can be the source of irritation and tension in any relationship.

In psychotherapy, as in other areas of intense personal interaction, the question is not whether transference reactions will take place—they most assuredly will—but what the parties to the relationship will do when the signs of transference show themselves. In the context of a transference relationship, the parental skills and attitudes of the therapist are put to the test. Practitioners of different therapy modalities handle transference in different ways. The most distinctive feature of psychoanalysis is the way it promotes the development of transference reactions and then seeks systematically to work them through in the cooperative effort of patient and analyst until the patient discovers their inappropriateness and is able clearly to separate the past from the present, to distinguish between his or her parents and the analyst, and to give up the once necessary but now inappropriate behaviors of childhood in favor of those which work satisfactorily in adulthood. In contrast to psychoanalysis, which is extended over time, the various brief therapy methods seek to prevent, bypass, or override the client's transference expectations; simply to set a time limit on the therapy may forestall the build-up of a strong transference relationship with its dependency, antagonism, or sexual arousal.

Therapists who work with clients in groups arrange a social setting in which transference feelings that might be directed toward themselves are diluted or dispersed by the interaction among group members. When Fritz Perls, the originator of Gestalt therapy, sensed that one of the members of a therapy group was wanting to be taken care of, he would typically instruct that person to "put your version of Fritz in that empty chair! Now tell him what you want from him." By declining to be "helpful," Perls prodded people toward confronting their own dependency and demandingness and to discover their own resources for self-direction. In his work with Nancy reported earlier, Russell Osnes was both directive and nurturant in a parental way. He encouraged Nancy to reexperience a painful scene from her past, held her hand when she chose to do so, accompanied her through the encounter with her father, then gave her opportunity to ask from others for what she felt she needed. When she chose to ask her husband to hold her, her wish for good fathering was shifted from the past to the present and deflected away from the therapist toward her mate.

A key question has to do with how much the therapist is willing to become the focus of the client's transference reactions and is prepared to work through those reactions in an effective way. Fritz Perls' biographer, Martin Shepard, has commented, "Fritz wanted, but wouldn't ask. And so he condemned the wantingness of others."[19] Gestalt therapy seeks directly to replace "wantingness," a useful colloquialism for transference, with individual responsibility. In contrast, Moe and Jacqui Lee Schiff have been willing to gratify their children's wantingness so as to lay the groundwork for recovery and maturity. Believing that parental responsiveness precedes child responsibility, the Schiffs sought as fully as possible to be the good mother and good father their children needed in order to become adults. They intended to achieve what Eric Berne once called a "transference cure," which "means the substitution of the therapist for the original parent, and . . . signifies that the therapist permits the patient to resume with him a game that was broken off in childhood by the untimely death or departure of the original parent, or else offers to play the game in a more benign form than the original parent did or does."[20]

Berne's suggestion that therapists can play games, too— *i.e.*, that therapists sometimes engage with their patients in repetitive patterns of interaction that lead to predictable consequences, happy or unhappy, for both of them—opens up the issue of countertransference. Technically, countertransference arises when the therapist expresses toward the client repressed feelings or tendencies out of his or her own earlier experience.

> Errors due to countertransference arise when the analyst reacts to his patient as though the patient were a significant person in the analyst's early history. . . . Countertransference reactions can lead to persistent inappropriate behavior toward the patient in the form of constant misunderstanding or some unconscious rewarding, seductive or permissive behavior of the analyst.[21]

Part of the continuing process of learning for the counselor or therapist goes on in consultation sessions with a supervisor or colleague. The work there includes uncovering and correcting the counselor's countertransference responses to his or her client, those ways in which the counselor sees in the client, without recognition, someone else out of the past. When countertransference continues unacknowledged the resultant misunderstanding may lead to dull routineness in the sessions, to angry confrontation or sullen passivity, or to sexual intimacy between therapist and client. It is essential for the therapist to know the games he likes to play with clients and to have ways to stop them and stay out of them when they are played for the client to lose.

The people who come to us for professional help frequently, if not usually, treat us like parents whether we want them to or not. We do not have the power to control their ways of seeing us, reaching out to us, or resisting us. Our choices arise in the selection of ways to respond to their expectations. We may ignore their transference reactions or reject them, divert them, explain them, gratify them literally and directly, exploit them to fulfill unmet needs of our own, or react the way our parents did when we were children and wanted something from them. Or we may act with awareness and purposefulness, choosing sometimes to be deliberately parental with the intention of enabling the client to become alive, more whole, more human. Part of our task is to see to it that psychotherapeutic reparenting is not simply countertransference error, an old game with new players.

Daughter-Clients, Father-Therapists?

The relationship between men psychotherapists and woman patients is a particularly intricate and complex one and has been so from the days of Freud's early collaboration with Josef Breuer in the use of hynotherapy in relieving the symptoms of women hysterics. Breuer had withdrawn from their investigations as a consequence of his discomfort when his famous patient "Anna O." had gone into the throes of a phantom childbirth on the day that Breuer had terminated the treatment in response to his wife's jealousy of his involvement with the patient. In due course Freud came to suspect that the efficacy of psychological treatment depended less upon technique than upon the personal relationship between the patient and her physician.

> Freud's suspicion was confirmed when, one day, a patient awoke from a hypnotic sleep and suddenly threw her arms around his neck. . . . Fortunately, unlike Breuer, he was not frightened by this experience. Rather, it aroused his scientific interest.[22]

And thus, it might be said, Freud discovered the phenomenon of transference.

The whole matter of the relations between the sexes in psychotherapy has been under careful scrutiny by women active in the feminist movement in their efforts to be free of the restrictive patriarchalism of our society's institutions. The book *Women and Madness* by Phyllis Chesler is a powerful and disconcerting indictment of the American mental health care system for its persistent subjugation of women to traditional male authority and values.[23] Feminists have raised the question whether at this point in the social history of women any man can provide adequate counseling for women. The feminists make a persuasive case for the view that many of women's problems are caused "by the warped and destructive cultural expectations we live with rather than by an unchangeable sickness from within."[24]

An appropriately feminist therapist has been described in one handbook for women in transition as someone who "makes no assumptions that there is a single proper role for women, and that she works hard to dispel the myths and stereotypes . . . which are so often used to justify the oppression of women."[25] The editors advise women to look for therapists who maintain an egalitarian style, who are open to their own inner experiencing, who are alert to the special issues which women face today, and who have struggled for their own freedom and identity as women and as persons.

> At the present we are making referrals to women therapists only. We do this for two reasons. The most important is that we feel it is much easier to trust a woman therapist's under-standings of women's problems than a man's. The entire profession is riddled with the assumptions of a male-dominated society about the nature of women.[26]

Phyllis Chesler has dedicated the major portion of her book on women "to the Daddy's girls we were—and are no longer." Chesler writes in a serious effort to achieve a definition of female sexuality that is not based on submission, powerlessness, dependency, and the deprivation of nurturant love. She has characterized the usual pattern of one-to-one psychotherapy in which troubled women seek help from professional men as one more outstanding example of "the rape-incest-procreation model of female sexuality."

> While most women do not commit incest with their biological fathers, patriarchal marriage, prostitution, and mass "romantic" love are psychologically predicated on sexual union between Daughter and Father figures.
>   The *sine qua non* of "feminine" identity in patriarchal society is the violation of the incest taboo, *i.e.*, the initial and continued "preference" for Daddy, followed by the approved falling in love with and/or marrying of powerful father figures. There is no real questioning of such feminine identity in psychotherapy. More often, an adjustment to it is preached— through verbal or sexual methods.[27]

Referring back to the original case illustrations based on Ralph Greenson's psychoanalytic work with Mrs. K. and on Russell Osnes spot reparenting of Nancy, a critical feminist might point to each outcome as an instance where a male therapist has delivered his female client over to a socially acceptable role of the wife who finds security and fulfillment in the care of her dependable father-figure husband.

Chesler, along with others, has raised the special question of sexual intimacy between therapist and patient. Love affairs between analysts and their women patients, sometimes leading to marriages, have not been a rarity in the history of modern psychotherapy.[28] The same might probably be said of the relations between men who are doctors or priests or lawyers or teachers and the women who seek their services and pay their fees. In her study of fifty-four women who had been psychiatrically treated in a hospital or in private therapy, Chesler discovered eleven women, about 20 percent of her sample, who told her of having had sexual relations with their male therapists, including two women who had been intimate with the same analyst.[29]

On occasion sexual intercourse between client and therapist has been proposed as a valid treatment method, although among professional psychologists, psychiatrists, marriage counselors, and others there is a broad consensus opposing that view. Recently West Coast newspapers carried the account of disciplinary charges brought against a well-known psychologist, "whose innovative therapy admittedly included sleeping with twelve female patients and taking nude photos of several of them." The action was brought against him on the complaint of a former female client. A friendly witness said that she had willingly had sexual relations with the therapist about once a week during a three-year period at the cost of two hundred and fifty dollars per month.[30] The state examining board suspended the psychologist's license.

In any discussion of man–woman relations in psychotherapy two separate issues become intertwined. One is that of cultural chauvinism, the acting out by both the male and female players of stereotyped sex roles. The second man–woman issue has to do with biological maleness and femaleness, with basic *sexuality* and not simply with ideological *sexism*. These same two issues pertain to relations between fathers and daughters in the family. There are signs of an increasingly determined effort to teach parents to be aware of and to change the attitudes within the family towards how boys and men, girls and women are supposed to feel, think, and act. In *Father Power*, Henry Biller and Dennis Meredith insist, for example,

> that fathers have a responsibility to help "turn the tide against society's tradition to resist socializing females for achievement."

> Fathers must recognize and value their daughters' verbal and physical aggressiveness as a legitimate basis for an abiding confidence and assertiveness in them.[31]

Along with learning to recognize and support his daughter's movement toward competence, independence, and active self-assertion, the effective father can learn to be comfortable with his own sexuality and with hers. Physical attraction between parents and children is one of the givens of an emotionally warm, relaxed family life. Feelings of affection and sensual pleasure need not be a source of fear or antagonism. The father who accepts his own maleness, who recognizes the sensual side of fatherhood, and who knows that natural sensuality does not lead to overt sexuality, is in a position to assist his daughter in coming to respect her own sensual nature and to enjoy closeness with him and with other persons, male and female, without anxiety.

Chesler has labeled sexual relations between a therapist and a client as "legally a form of rape and psychologically a form of incest."[32] The analogy between the incest taboo within the family and the prohibition of sexual relations between a male therapist and his female client is appropriate. Within the nuclear family system sexual relations are carefully regulated. One rule *pre*scribes, that is, endorses and provides for, sexual relations between the adult husband–wife partners. A second rule *pro*scribes overt sexual intimacy between any other family member pairs—between mother and son, brother and sister, father and daughter. Sociologists have suggested that this incest taboo, the prohibition of direct genital sexual expression between any except the partner-parents, serves a dual function. First, it protects the children against a kind and quality of physical contact for which they may be neither physiologically nor psychologically ready, thereby providing for that sense of security children need to develop properly. And second, the incest prohibition also serves to orient the sexually maturing child toward finding sexual gratification with partners outside of the family. The restriction on sex relations with the family "propels" the child out of the family in the direction of the formation of a new nuclear family and also into nonfamilial roles in the larger society.[33]

Translating the intention of the incest taboo into the psychotherpeutic setting, the prohibition of explicit sexual contact between a man therapist and a woman client, offers safety for the client as she may come to experience erotic feelings at a deep level. Also, in denying sexual satisfaction within the close alliance, the taboo requires the client to discover ways of achieving sensual pleasure and interpersonal intimacy in the larger social sphere. (The restriction also protects the therapist and necessitates *his* finding ways to meet his needs for contact and fulfillment in a "non-incestuous" way!) As in the family, the agreement, whether implied or explicit, between therapist and client not to have sexual relations allows them the freedom to be aware of whatever feelings they have for each other, to accept them, to discuss them when appropriate, and to channel them toward the client's therapeutic goals.

There is yet another facet of the whole matter of women in therapy to be touched on here, at least briefly. It might be summed up, "Women need mothering, too!" Phyllis Chesler argues that many women, perhaps most in our society, have been seriously deprived of adequate mothering in childhood as a result of the cultural preference for males. She believes that to compensate for this lack, women must deliberately find ways to give and receive nurturance with one another.[34] This would include the choice of women as therapists by women seeking help. In an interesting way, Chesler's view has affinity with an observation that psychoanalyst Ralph

Greenson has made about transference: "Eventually in a successful analysis the analyst should have become both a father and mother figure."[35] Greenson continues:

> It has been my clinical experience that my men patients have particularly strong resistance in experiencing toward me their oral-sadistic hatred toward the mother. On the other hand, my women patients seem to have unusual difficulty in resolving their resistance toward experiencing me as the loving, breast-giving mother figure.
>
> What is most difficult in men is the primitive hatred of mother; and in women the primitive love of mother.[36]

I perceive a growing need for more well-trained women in the field of mental health care and personal growth education. It makes sense to expect a woman therapist to be especially prepared to deal with the deep resistances to work through primitive feelings toward mother figures that Greenson has identified as well as to provide the active remothering of clients that the therapy may sometimes call for. While I recognize that my task may include refathering, increasingly I find myself at some stage referring women who come to me for help to other women, whether for therapy or consciousness-raising or assertiveness-training or for the sharing of sisterhood. As we professionals learn more about doing psychotherapeutic reparenting, we are likely to rely more heavily on the man–woman co-therapy model to give breadth and balance to our efforts. I appreciate the correctness of the feminists' insistence that biological differences between men and women must no longer be used as excuse for the suppression of women in any area of life. At the same time, in our thinking about parenting and about psychotherapy, we must seek to understand and appreciate the reality, the force, and the value of the energies derived from those same biological differences.

Beyond Fathering

"To be a father one need not sire a biological offspring. Fatherhood is being a sensitive friend to a child, and by this standard there are too few fathers."[37]

As I read the literature on good parenting and effective psychotherapy, I find the same qualities and functions attributed to both sets of caretaking behaviors. There is a consensus that the nature of the relationship between father and child or between therapist and client influences the outcome of the work more than specific techniques. Consider some of the words used repeatedly to characterize what effective parents and therapists *do* and how they *are* as persons.

An effective parent or a proficient therapist,
at appropriate times and in appropriate ways,

protects,	touches,	encourages,
nurtures,	talks,	permits,
accepts,	looks,	cares,
stimulates,	listens,	stays available,
limits,	understands,	releases.

Both do their best work when they are

self-aware,	sensitive,	flexible,
self-accepting,	empathic,	responsible,
congruent,	expressive,	knowledgeable,
independent,	committed,	powerful.

These characteristics pertain equally to men and women, to fathers and mothers. In attending to children, a father is capable of gentleness, tenderness, emotionality, and nurturance; a mother can be independent, informed, and strong. Each brings to parenting unique individuality, specialized experience with the culturally defined masculine and

feminine roles, and his or her basic sexuality. The matter of
authority, or power, deserves special comment. It is necessary not to invoke traditional authoritarianism in advocating
good fathering (and mothering) in family life and in
professional caregiving. Biller and Meredith take pains to
declare that father power is not the same thing as pater-
nalism.

> By father power we do *not* mean power to be used over
> children, tyrannical power, or paternalistic power. Rather we
> mean the pervasive, profound power that is a part of your and
> every other father's nature as a parent. Paternalism is the use of
> masculine power to shape a person into something the
> paternalist thinks he should be, regardless of the wants of the
> person. Father power is the use of your profound, natural
> influence to help your child become what he wants to be. You
> not only teach your child what he will need to know to prosper
> in the world, but you also give him an important sense of
> independence from you—his own sense of power.[38]

Erica Jong's novel *Fear of Flying* is the story of a woman's
journey into self-acceptance. For Isadora, the protagonist-
narrator, the way to her own truth led through a world
populated with psychoanalysts. Early in her journal, Isadora
describes her final session with Dr. Kolner, the last in the
array of six analysts with whom she had had treatment.
Isadora had begun to question Kolner's right to tell her who
she was. She suspected that her mistrust of him was not just
her problem but was based on an accurate reading of him.
She dared to challenge him.

> "I don't believe what you believe," I yelled, "and I don't
> respect your beliefs and I don't respect you for holding them. I
> don't want to live by the things you live by. I don't want that
> kind of life and I can't see why I should be judged by its
> standards. I also don't think you understand a thing about
> women." "Maybe you don't understand what it means to be a
> woman," he countered.

They plunged on in an uproar. Isadora insulted the doctor, raged at him for his "small-man complex," until the analyst was provoked to retort, "You ought to quit if you feel that way about me. Leave. Walk out. Slam the door. Tell me to go to hell."

Isadora kept the argument going a bit longer, struggling to persuade Kolner of the absurdity of psychoanalysis. Again he countered, "I can only reiterate what I said before. If you don't like it why don't you just get the hell out."

And she did.

> As in a dream (I never would have believed myself capable of it) I got up from the couch (how many years had I been lying there?), picked up my pocketbook, and walked (no, I did not quite "saunter"—though I wish I had) out the door. I closed it gently . . . Goodbye, Kolner.[39]

For 280 more pages, Isadora details her childhood, her fantasies, her poetry writing, her attendance at an international psychoanalytic congress in Vienna. She separates from her analyst husband Bennett, plays out an affair with another analyst, Adrian, and declines the chance to act out her dreams of anonymous sex without involvement. In the end she has come to a single, clear decision. "I was determined to take my fate in my own hands. . . . I was going to stop being a school girl."

In the book's last scene Isadora lies stretched out in a deep, claw-footed bathtub in an old London hotel room, wondering if Bennett will come to find her there.

> I hadn't the remotest idea of what was going to happen next and for the moment I didn't care. I floated lightly in the deep tub, feeling that something was different, something was strange, but I couldn't figure out just what it was. I looked down at my body. The same. . . . A nice body. Mine. I decided to keep it. I hugged myself. It was my fear that was missing.

> The cold stone I had worn inside my chest for twenty-nine years was gone. Not suddenly. And maybe not for good. But it was gone. . . .
> Whatever happened, I knew I would survive it. I knew, above all, that I'd go on working. Surviving meant being born over and over. It wasn't easy, and it was always painful. But there wasn't any other choice except death.

> Isadora speculates about what she will say, how she will act, if Bennett walks in and discovers her there in his room. 'If you grovel, you'll be back at square one,' Adrian had said. I knew for sure I wasn't going to grovel. But that was all I knew. It was enough."[40]

Many women have read *Fear of Flying* as their own story of the quest for selfhood. It is a modern parable of growing up female and an oblique commentary on psychoanalysis as well.

Jay Haley, who has written extensively about the dynamics of psychotherapy, once defined psychoanalysis as

> a dynamic psychological process involving two people, a patient and a psychoanalyst, during which the patient insists that the analyst be one-up while desperately trying to place him one-down, and the analyst insists that the patient remain one-down in order to help him learn to become one-up. The goal of the relationship is the amicable separation of analyst and patient.[41]

With Haley's definition in mind, we may look back from the scene of Isadora in the bathtub to that earlier moment of her tempestuous farewell to Dr. Kolner and appreciate the ironic connection. Irascible chauvinist that he was, with his Freudian interpretations and "warmed-over clichés about women's place," Kolner had nevertheless carried out his professional task! He had provoked Isadora into leaving for good. Not only did she end her arrangement with Kolner, but she gave up any further attempt to gain anything from psychoanalysis. Though their separation was hardly amicable, Kolner had done his job!

Psychotherapist and author Sheldon Kopp, tracing the pilgrimage of the client in therapy, has written,

> The psychotherapy patient must . . . come to this heavy piece of understanding, that he does *not* need the therapist. The most important things that each man must learn, no one else can teach him. . . . Unwilling to tolerate life's ambiguity, its inevitability, we search for certainty, demanding that someone else must provide it. Stubbornly, relentlessly, we seek the wise man, the wizard, the good parent, someone else who will show us the way.
>
> But what if we are talking to ourselves? What if there is no one out there listening? What if for each of us the only wise man, the only wizard, the only good parent we will ever have is our own helpless, vulnerable self? What then?[42]

That same "heavy piece of understanding" awaits the child-becoming-adult: he or she does not need parents. In parenting, a set of persons who are identified as grown-ups work hard at interacting with another set of persons identified as not-grown-ups, controlling them in such a way that they learn to take control of themselves, caring for them so that they become their own caretakers. When parenting is successful, the child discovers, after fifteen or twenty years of living with father and mother in unequal relationship, that he or she and they are, in truth, equals. Then he or she leaves home, perhaps later to return as a visiting friend.

Both parents and psychotherapists engage in the craft or art of what family therapist Virginia Satir has aptly called "peoplemaking."[43] Both have the task of dealing with others in ways that allow for the development of what they are naturally ready for—for the healing of hurts, the enrichment of consciousness, the release of energies, the movement of human life toward individuality, integrity, love, and wisdom. Some things a person can only do for himself or herself. No one gives another freedom. Once when I was thoroughly frustrated with myself and a woman with whom I had been counseling over a long period, about whom I cared, and to whom I felt too tightly bound at that moment, I wrote in my notes:

"I will achieve more of my freedom when I have allowed you, led you, tricked you, or propelled you toward your own. And I know now that I cannot simply hand freedom over to you, even when I want to (and sometimes I don't!). I intend to recover my sense of independence. What you do is up to you. I can and will stop leaning on you, rescuing you, hassling you, taking care of you. I can let go and will. But I don't have the power to give you your power. You already have it. The issue is not whether I will or won't permit you to be free and strong, but only whether, and when, you will start to use the freedom and strength you already have."

In his book *If You Meet the Buddha on the Road, Kill Him!* Kopp explains that the title is intended to point up

that no meaning that comes from outside of ourselves is real. The Buddhahood of each of us has already been obtained. We need only recognize it. . . . Killing the Buddha on the road means destroying the hope that anything outside of ourselves can be our master. No one is any bigger than anyone else. There are no mothers or fathers for grown-ups, only sisters and brothers.[44]

"No mothers or fathers for grown-ups, only sisters and brothers": These words capture for me the meaning of my career goal as a father and as a psychotherapist. Without fathers and mothers there are no children to become brothers and sisters. But fathering and mothering are time-limited vocations. Beyond parenting lie other opportunities for adventure and growth in becoming persons. For men who are fathers—biologically, psychologically, socially—there is liberation when we have been adept in carrying out our tasks. Our children leave us and then we and they are free to reunite as companionable equals or to go our separate ways.

Chapter VII

Creative Fathering: The Problems and Potentialities of Changing Sex Roles

Howard Clinebell

Profound changes are occurring in the way the two halves of the human family—the female and the male halves—are treating each other. The most obvious expression of these changes is the women's liberation movement. But in a wider perspective, the changes reflect a struggle for *human* liberation, the freeing of both women and men from life-constricting cultural stereotypes and institutional sexism. A major metamorphasis in human consciousness and identity is occurring in our segment of history.

The women's and men's liberation movements are the most basic of the many liberation struggles of our time because they will eventually have an impact on everyone and because they have the most direct and powerful influence on the key people-forming institution, the family. Consequently, the human liberation movement has precipitated a severe crisis in parenting.

For fathers and prospective fathers, the deep changes in sex roles and identities are causing unprecedented pressures and problems. But the changes are also creating unprecedented resources and possibilities for more creative fathering. My intent is to describe the problems and then focus on how we can respond constructively to this crisis in fathering, both as individuals and in our institutions.

For many centuries, traditional male–female relationship patterns have limited most women to a satellite identity—an identity derived from their relationship with a man (or the lack of such a relationship in the case of a single woman). Derivative identities are inherently partial and inferior to that upon which they are dependent. The derivative identities of women have been associated with severe inequalities of opportunity to develop their full potential. Now, in a rising wave of awareness, more and more women are rejecting their derivative identity and insisting on their right to full equality.

Perhaps a science fiction parable will communicate what many men are experiencing as women change. Imagine that a star, through some stellar catastrophy, lost its major satellite. This proved to be an astronomical trauma, throwing the star wobbling into a strange orbit. These events revealed how dependent the star had been on the satellite's dependency in order to stay in its own central position. To make matters more disturbing, the ex-satellite then becomes a star in its own right, with its own space and orbit of power.

My parable does violence to the realities of astronomy, but it is accurate in symbolizing what many of us males have experienced emotionally as the most important woman in our life broke out of her satellite orbit. To change the figure of speech, for me the change was something like being on the top of a seesaw when the person on the bottom gets off suddenly and unexpectedly. It's jarring to one's security as well as one's anatomy. The changes in Charlotte have been threatening to me on a feeling level partly because I affirmed and encouraged them intellectually. The revision of her identity as a woman has forced me to become aware of and begin to revise my identity as a man.

The task of being an adequate parent is not easy in the best of circumstances. In a time of radical changes in the self-understanding of women and men, it is especially difficult. We are only in the early stages of sex-role liberation. It is reasonable to expect the impact of this struggle on parenting to increase significantly in the decades ahead. This makes it imperative that individual parents, couples, and leaders in people-serving institutions devise more constructive ways of coping with the escalating crisis of parenting.

Problems of Contemporary Fathers

Let's look at some of the pressures and dilemmas confronting fathers today. Behind all the problems there is an anxious uncertainty in many of us regarding the nature of our function and role. As I wrote this chapter, I became aware of more resistance and ambivalence than even the usual high level of those feelings that I have when I write. As I explored my feelings, I became aware of my sense of uncertainty and inadequacy in the area of being a father. Looking through a file on fatherhood, I found the notes from a talk I gave to a parents group a few years ago entitled "Making the Grade as Dad." I was appalled by some of the things I declared with conviction on that occasion, things I am convinced now are simply not true. Who am I to try to tell others where it's at in the area of fathering, particularly when what I see today will probably not be at all what I believe tomorrow? So, I must write with a spirit of tentativeness and with the hope that some of what follows will prove to be valid and useful to others who are also struggling to find paths to more creative fathering.

Many of us husbands are experiencing high anxiety precipitated by our wives' growing autonomy but actually caused by the necessity of updating our self-perception as men, husbands, and fathers. Revising one's identity produces strong anxiety whatever the life-stage or circumstance that makes it necessary. Furthermore, the anxiety of husbands and wives becomes mutually reinforcing as each goes through identity-revision struggles. Elevated anxiety in parents blunts their ability to respond with sensitivity to their children's emotional hungers.

Effective fathering is made more difficult today by the escalating marital conflict and hostility resulting as the wife demands more rapid change toward equality than the husband is willing to tolerate. This conflict often produces alienation and wastes enormous creative energy. This is because so many of us have not learned to resolve conflict in ways that deepen intimacy. Since most men feel that they have more to lose and less to gain in changing roles, their anger and grief levels are often high. Feeling deprived themselves, they suffer from diminished ability to hear and respond to their children's needs.

Men are programmed in our society to be "strong" and to ignore their feelings, particularly those labeled "weak." Their grief response to the losses caused by changing roles is often not recognized as grief. (The losses that men experience in changing roles include the loss of feelings of automatic superiority and status and of being served and supported by women.) Their grief wounds tend therefore to remain unhealed and to become infected by festering feelings of loss, anger, and deprivation. A bereaved father is less available or "present" to his child.

Fathers are getting it from all sides today. The sociologists remind us of our multifaceted inadequacies. If we are white and middle class, the women's movement reminds us that we are part of the largest existing group of "oppressed oppressors." Closer to home, a husband often becomes the target of chronic hostility from his wife as she becomes aware of the gross inequalities in the marriage and in our male dominated institutions. The media add their bit with the Dagwood Bumstead Syndrome.[1] It isn't easy to be an open, loving, giving father when you feel under siege.

The awareness that the critics of fathers are at least partly right increases our pain and defensiveness. The realistic guilt that so many fathers experience when we take an honest look at ourselves resonates to the ubiquitous criticism and makes it more difficult for us to function as constructive parents.

Another problem of contemporary fathers is the paucity of preparation for the role, coupled with a confusion or partial vacuum about just what the role is today. Most little girls have opportunities to learn mothering feelings and behavior through observing their mothers and by their play. But the way we raise boys deprives them of adequate opportunities to learn constructive fathering. They observe and internalize their father's attitudes and behavior, which are often detached, vague, and ambivalent. Lacking viable inner role models to guide them, many new fathers experience confusion and elevated anxiety in their role. Studies show that most fathers respond to the birth of their first child with much more anxiety than they did to the adjustments of marriage.[2]

Fathering identity diffusion has been enhanced by rapidly changing sex roles. Many of us reject the role models we internalized from our fathers because we feel they are no longer viable particularly in egalitarian marriages. As one young adult father said in a marriage enrichment group, "I don't want to be with my two kids the way dad was with me, but it's tough as hell to find out how I *do* want to be. As a father, I'm really flying by the seat of my pants!" It's an anxiety-laden journey to walk in a strange land with no map.

For most parents, the accelerating speed of social change widens the generation gap in both directions—with their children and with their own parents. This reduction in the security-giving continuity of the generations contributes to the loneliness and sense of loss many parents feel. We know that our children have grown up in a different world and that they must learn new ways to cope with an even more radically different future. Therefore there can be less of the validation of us as parents and less of the reduction of our anxiety about dying that comes from seeing one's values and life-style continued in our children.

Societal programming exerts relentless contradictory pressures on middle-class males, putting them in a double bind. One pressure is to support a family and "get ahead." The other is to get more involved in family life including child nurture. This pressure is reinforced by the criticism of wives, the admonition of child-rearing specialists, and our own needs for close relationships. Over-investment in one's job often is a male cop-out from family involvement. It must be recognized, however, that society greases the slope down which men slide into work addiction and the progressive, painful isolation from relationships that results.

The disintegration of some one million marriages each year in the United State leaves many fathers even more physically and emotionally detached from their children. Divorced, part-time fathers are deprived of many of the responsibilities and satisfactions that resident parents have in relationship to their children. The increasing economic and emotional freedom of women and the chaos of changing roles will cause the divorce rate to continue to rise in the decades ahead. Even when marital dissolution clearly is better for all concerned, new and different problems inevitably emerge for both fathers and mothers.

Potentialities for More Creative Fathering

Alongside the complex problems described above, there exist a new set of possibilities for more mutually rewarding relationships between dads and children. As a father whose progeny are young adults, out of the nest, this awareness brings me a certain sadness. A part of me would like the chance to go back and do it differently the second time around. (A part of me also knows that if I had the chance, I would make many of the same mistakes again, plus some new ones.)

Let's look at some new parameters of parenting for fathers. The most important and valuable possibility is that of developing closer, more open, and mutually fulfilling relationships between dads and children than usually occur when men regard breadwinning and linking the family with the outside world as their major roles. Regular involvement in the grubby, sometimes satisfying work of caring for children increases the opportunity to experience the satisfactions of contributing to their unfolding personhood. I felt a twinge of regret not long ago as I watched a young father push a baby carriage across the street in front of our school and remembered my own nearly total absorption in graduate school and work when our children were very small.

One father describes the change that has occurred as he has shared child nurturing more evenly with his wife: "My fathering has always taken the form of a friendly cloud that floated across the lives of the children, and paused occasionally to cast a shadow. That they would turn out to have their own weather, and that I would profit by the climate, was an immense satisfaction."[3]

Fathers also have the opportunity today for more mutually fulfilling marriages. There are two priceless gifts we can give our children. One is the gift of relating to them as authentic, growing persons; the other is relating to our spouse in a growing, loving way. Couples who have the patience, courage, and resources to ride out the initial storm of changing roles often find a fresh, better-than-ever chapter opening in their marriages. An enlivened marriage offers an optimal interpersonal environment for children to discover their own full potential.

As couples share parenting and work-for-pay, fathers often gain relief from the heavy breadwinning responsibilities and more time to relate to themselves, their spouses, and their children. Furthermore, reducing the male success race pressure may help men stay alive longer and thus have more time for enjoying their children as well as their grandchildren.

Dads today have an opportunity to help develop more creative styles of fathering than were possible in traditional societies. This kind of relational pioneering is an exciting possibility more available to fathers today than ever before.

Research confirms what some dads have always known intuitively, that children grow best when they have fathers (as well as mothers) who combine strength, limit-setting, and protection, on the one hand, with warmth and nurturing on the other. One study showed that "loving fathers who direct their children's activities in a rational, issue-oriented way . . . promote competence in their children."[4] Other studies have shown that boys whose fathers give warm affection and nurture, as well as provide discipline, are least likely to have problems with their masculine identity. Children of either sex who receive both types of caring from their fathers, as well as their mothers, are most likely to become generous, morally sensitive, and creative sons or daughters.[5]

How Can Fathers Be More Creative?

The growth perspective is the most useful orientation for enhancing relationships with our children. This perspective is like a set of glasses through which one sees people in terms of what they can become and thus helps them to become. There is an undiscovered gold mine of intelligence, creativity, and possibilities for living life more fully, usefully, and joyfully in ourselves, our children, and our spouses. Creative fathering occurs in a family in which everyone is free to grow using more of her or his God-given possibilities. Liberation is *from* whatever blocks the use of our gifts and *to* what the New Testament describes as "life in all its fullness" (John 10:10 NEB). The major cost for men (as for women) in conforming to narrow sex-role stereotypes is unlived life. The positive challenge of changing roles is to throw off imprisoning stereotypes and become the fuller human beings we have the gifts to become.

There are three interdependent levels of liberation, understood as growth potentializing, each of which has implications for creative fathering:

1) *Inner liberation:* The most basic contribution a father can make to his children's growth is to get out of the male trap of the machismo mystique.[6] Liberation is contagious. To the extent that a father is an open, growing person, his children will tend to "catch" and internalize his liberated attitudes and ways of relating.

Just what is the male trap? As an illustration, let me describe mine. My trap includes my work addiction and the compulsion to achieve; overvaluing my competitive side and over-commitment to the scramble for status and achievement; ignoring and neglecting my softer feelings because they have felt "unmasculine"; pushing so intensely for future goals that I am unaware in the present moment; neglecting relationships that do not serve my efforts to "get ahead"; not allowing myself adequate time to relax and enjoy fully things like playing the French horn or sitting in the sun; letting the urgent things push out the important things in my life (Robert Hutchins); being controlled by the oughts and the shoulds; not drinking deeply of the stream of my experiences of myself, nature, people, and Spirit.

I find that getting out of this trap even temporarily isn't easy. The trap feels so normal, so "right," so seductively rewarding. But in my freer, more aware moments, I sense the exorbitant cost of this life-style to me and the way it diminishes my relations with the people I really care about.

To gain liberation from the male box, and thus to have more to bring to fathering, requires men to affirm their rejected or neglected side—the soft, nurturing, vulnerable, feelingful, needing-people side that our culture has brainwashed us to define as "unmasculine." The truth, which many of us are discovering, is that this definition is a tragically impoverished conception of masculinity. Learning to say yes to this side of himself gives a man a stronger, richer, more balanced and whole masculine identity.

What are some of the steps one can take to revise and liberate one's identity? There are no easy answers, but let me suggest some things that help me.

One thing is to recognize clearly that my inner trap is my own creation, maintained by my current feelings, attitudes, and behavior. The trap is reinforced by my relationships and my institutional context, but, in the final analysis, it continues only as I re-create it every day by my choices.

Therefore, I have the power to choose more liberating options. No one else can liberate me, and I cannot liberate anyone else from his or her inner entrapment.

Another freeing insight is that I must want more inner liberation for myself (rather than primarily to please or satisfy others). The awareness of the price one pays by remaining captive to the male mystique and the positive satisfactions of liberation are prime motivators of action to change one's inner life.

It may be helpful to the reader to write out a balance sheet of profits and losses resulting from being locked in the male game, gains and losses of the things that are important to you, *e.g.*, health, relationships, enjoyment, creativity, longevity, and so forth. How many years would you estimate your present life-style is deducting from your life expectancy? (If you're on the male success treadmill, a decade is probably a very conservative estimate.)

Inner liberation can be facilitated by exposing oneself to consciousness-raising periodicals, such as *Ms.* magazine, or to a consciousness-raising book such as *The American Male* by Myron Brenton, *The Male Dilemma* by Anne Steinmann and David J. Fox, *The Male Machine* by Marc F. Fasteau, or *Meet Me in the Middle* by Charlotte H. Clinebell. I experience self-confrontation when I read these authors' analyses of the male box and their suggestions concerning the path out.

Few things are more helpful in one's inner liberation struggles than participating regularly in a men's consciousness-raising (CR) group. Such groups can be of tremendous benefit to men who are feeling shaken by their wives' changing identities. In such a group, one can experience the "growth formula," that blend of support, understanding, and caring, on the one hand, and honesty and confrontation on the other that most stimulates growth. A liberation or CR group provides an interpersonal environment that encourages, supports, and rewards liberating attitudes and behaviors.[7] Joining the local chapter of N.O.W. (the National Organization for Women) is one thing a father can do to raise his own consciousness and find a support group of other men struggling for personal, relational, and institutional liberation.

Inner liberation is aided by choosing to *do* the things that will enrich your inner world and relationships and help you use more of your whole self. One of our sons ended a letter recently with this three-word suggestion: "Smell a flower!" Not bad advice. (It is encouraging to know that our children are often more liberated than we are and that we can catch liberating attitudes and behavior from them. It can be reassuring as well as disconcerting to discover that one's children have liberated themselves in spite of, as much as because of, the ways we raised them.)

Centering is another practice that can aid inner liberation. This involves interrupting the hectic pace, putting on the brakes, and taking time to reclaim one's inner space. Having slowed down, the next step is to explore one's own consciousness with no goal except heightened awareness. Centering can be described as opening myself to whatever I am experiencing in this particular moment. It is not *struggling* for greater awareness. As I explore my consciousness, I become aware of the varied feelings and unused resources of my inner world, including my so-called soft side.

In transactional analysis language, inner liberation can be described as freeing my inner Child from the control of my prejudicial Parent, allowing my nurturing Parent to give my Child more loving and caring, and then turning on my Adult. When Charlotte began to move out of her satellite identity, my Child reacted with feelings of anger, fear, and deprivation. Gradually my Adult became aware of what was happening within. I began to sense the ways in which I had hidden my Child needs from myself by playing Parent with Charlotte, at the same time I was getting Child gratification by her mothering of me. I have observed similar patterns in other men in counseling and enrichment groups. Responses of unreasonable fears and anger often are triggered by the wife's legitimate request for more autonomy and opportunity.

Awareness of these tranactions increases one's ability to choose whether or not to allow old Child and Parent recordings to control one's current behavior. If a father is to respond more creatively to his children, he must discover what messages his inner Father and Mother and Child tapes are playing to him. He can then choose to initiate new behavior that gradually will reprogram his parenting feelings and responses.

2) *Liberating our Relationship:* Inner liberation is reciprocally related to liberating one's intimate relationships with one's spouse and children. One couple in a marriage enrichment weekend reported in the evaluation at the end, "We discovered here how we have encouraged each other to stay boxed in and some ways we can support each other in getting out of the damn boxes." Neurotic marital interaction is a process of mutual strangulation of each other's growth. In contrast, the essence of liberating love (which is the same as authentic Christian love) is commitment to growth—one's own and each other's. If I love you, I really care about what helps you grow.

How can a couple increase the degree of mutual growth in their relationship? The basic strategy is to adopt an *intentional marriage* style. This is the opposite of drifting and hoping things will improve. It is liberating to discover that together we can make an ordinary or good marriage better by rewriting the obsolete, non-growth-producing clauses in our marriage covenant. The Intentional Marriage Method, which I have described elsewhere, is a do-it-yourself tool for accomplishing this.[8] (The majority of couples with whom we have worked in marriage enrichment workshops have reported that the Intentional Marriage Method is the most practical communication and conflict-resolution tool they learned during the events.) Couples who want more mutually liberating relationships can plan and do those things now that will help them create a better future.

A new style of marriage is emerging particularly among young adults. This is the *potentializing marriage* in which mutual growth is the central dynamic of the relationship. Studies of young adult marriages show that both women and men are asking increasingly for a deepening intimacy within which mutual growth will occur.[9] Genuine self-fulfillment requires self-other fulfillment in a relationship of mutual growth. Thus, the goal of a potentializing marriage is creative interdependency. It helps couples liberate their relationships to work intentionally toward a more potentializing marriage.

Nothing can be more liberating to children than experiencing a growing relationship between their parents. For children to "catch" (internalize) this model of how men and women relate is the most valuable preparation for their own future marriages.

To redesign a marriage relationship requires learning new communication skills, particularly the skills of renegotiating a more just division of the satisfactions and drudgeries and the skills of resolving conflict between equals. Since changing roles means more *open* conflict, it is crucial to learn better ways of resolving these. Resolving conflict between equals is a different and more difficult process than resolving conflict in a one-up/one-down relationship. The differences require the skills of negotiating a just way of satisfying some of the needs of both parties.

Achieving a more liberating marriage is facilitated by having a sharing group in which couples can give each other support, feedback, and caring confrontation. More creative marriages are possible today than ever before because the best form of intimacy is between equals who respect each other and prize each other's growth. But to realize this possibility most couples need a caring community to help them discover their own unique style of marital creativity. We have found it difficult to maintain such a sharing group of couples but well worth the effort it takes.

For us and for most of the couples we know, relational liberation began with the woman's rising consciousness. Charlotte's moves to liberate herself gave me my first inkling that I might need liberating too. For this I am deeply grateful to her. The chain reaction in the family organism that eventually leads to a more liberated father–child relationship may have to begin by the wife-mother joining a CR group of women. Her raised consciousness will probably change the dynamics of the marriage and force the husband-father to begin to do something about liberating his side of that relationship. If he does this, it will eventually transform his relationship with his children. The parents, as "architects of the family" (Virginia Satir's phrase), can, by liberating themselves and their relationship, gradually liberate the family organism so that everyone will be freer to be and to become.

In addition to the steps described above, a father can enhance his relationships with his children by joining an enlightened parent's support and training group or a training group for expectant couples. The common practice of designing and scheduling parent education events for mothers must change if fathers are to make their vital contribution to children's growth. Every parental and preparental group should help raise awareness of the problems and possibilities of changing roles and encourage couples to design innovative approaches to shared parenting that will be most fulfilling to them and to their children.

3) *Liberating our institutions:* Our institutions too often frustrate rather than facilitate the growth of persons. For example, most institutions make it more difficult for fathers and mothers to break out of rigid sex-role stereotypes about the work they do. In their rules, customs, and policies, such institutions fossilize sexism.

A young couple I know decided before their first child was born to share the parenting and the breadwinning. This would allow both to continue their satisfying careers and to share the joys and responsibilities of their child. Most employing institutions make it difficult or impossible to implement such a plan. But they were fortunate. The wife, a psychotherapist, and the husband, a teacher, could each find half-time work. After their son was born, however, they received flack from various sources. The orthodox psychiatrists at the clinic where the wife worked made dire predictions about how their son's sexual identity would be confused by their sharing the nurturing and breadwinning roles. One grandmother raised an objection, stating that their baby would be deprived of the mother's full-time care—the kind that "only a mother can give." Fortunately both parents knew that each could give warm nurture to their son and both were convinced that the crucial variable in their son's sexual identity formation was their affirmation of their own maleness and femaleness respectively. So they resisted the pressure that might have caused a less secure couple to retreat into traditional roles. It would take much less courage and determination to try more satisfying patterns of shared parenting if our institutions modified themselves to encourage flexible experimentation.

A change that is sorely needed in both businesses and the military is to reduce and eventually eliminate the practices that separate fathers from their families for long periods. Studies of long-absent and missing fathers show that the effects often are destructive to the marriages and the children.[10] It's time our institutions stopped contributing to the widespread alienation of fathers and children.

On the positive side, the churches, schools, and social agencies in a community can help by creating a network of enrichment, consciousness-raising, and sharing groups to help parents cope constructively during this period of confusing change in interpersonal relationships. The ultimate goal of such a network of groups is to help these institutions to become better human development and wholeness centers, so that their constituents can maximize their growth. Here are some of the groups that can help prevent family disasters by fostering creative relationships.

—Consciousness-raising groups for women, for men, and for couples with a variety of sponsorship, labels, and formats.

—Marriage enrichment retreats, workshops, classes, and groups to help couples develop more mutually fulfilling relationships at each of the changing stages of marriage and parenthood.

—Preparation for parenthood classes and training groups for couples to help them learn the skills and devise a plan to share the nurture of their baby.

—Solo parents groups to provide mutual support and a substitute extended family within which children and adults can experience caring adults of both sexes.

—Creative singlehood group and divorce growth groups for men and women to help them help each other cope with the challenges of parenthood as singles. Such groups can help divorced persons work through their grief feelings so that their wounds can heal and their ability to be constructive parents be increased.

—Family clusters composed of several nuclear families plus some singles to work together to develop their families as environments for mutual growth.[11] One value of such a cluster is the opportunity for fathers to empathize, support, and learn from each other.

Implications for Counseling with Fathers

For those of us who work with fathers in counseling or marriage enrichment events, the profound changes in women's and men's identities have these urgent implications:

It is important to make sure that our counseling and enrichment work is liberating (in the sense of potentializing.) I recall a counseling relationship with a depressed middle-aged man, in which unwittingly I contributed to his staying trapped in the male box, because my own awareness had not been raised at that point. He had a job that demanded so much of his time and energy that he had little left for his relationships with his family. This produced painful problems in his marriage. I tried to help him resolve his anger, but I missed the sense of unlived life that must have been at the root of his anger and depression. It probably would have helped him more if he had become more angry about his job and more aware of the way he was selling his soul to it because of his programming as a man. A basic reexamination of the distorted priorities that his exorbitant sense of male responsibilities caused him to embrace might have encouraged him to change his job or at least his over-investment in it. I could give comparable examples of counseling experiences with women in which the effect was to encourage them to adjust to a one-down marriage relationship, rather than helping them become aware that this was the basic problem about which they must do something to be able to be more alive and fulfilled as persons.

In counseling with troubled marriages it is particularly critical to explore the possibility that a basic reason why the couples are caught in conflict or boredom is that they are locked in sex-role stereotypes that prevent one or both from using their potential.

In a time of change and often chaos in sex roles, it is important to understand that relational counseling is essentially coaching in relationship skills. More creative marriage and parenthood require learning new communication skills, as has been suggested above. In many cases men have been particularly deprived of early opportunities to learn relationship-building skills. Effective counseling and relationship enrichment can help to provide this remedial skill training.

Growth counseling philosophy emphasizes that a stronger commitment in the helping professions to *prevention* through marriage and family enrichment is essential.[12] Investing at least as much of our professional energy in positive prevention by family enrichment events as in the repair work of counseling is imperative if we are to help couples cope constructively with changing roles!

If a counselor or enrichment facilitator is to help raise the consciousness of clients, it is essential that he or she first experience consciousness raising. This should include an examination of the sexism that may still be affecting his or her own intimate relationships. For those of us who train counselors, it is important that we recruit more women for training and involve all trainees in CR experiences.

Marriage counseling and enrichment events should, whenever possible, involve male–female co-leadership. Psychotherapy and counseling have traditionally been deeply infected with male chauvinist attitudes, prejudices, and practices.[13] Liberating the counseling and marriage enrichment fields deserves top priority in attention of us practitioners. This cannot occur until we have a better balance between women and men in the counseling professions and among those who do the clinical and academic training of counselors. It is also crucial to eliminate sexist language (language that excludes women) from our writing and speaking in the counseling disciplines.

For those of us who work within the context of churches, or who have a special interest in spiritual liberation and growth, it is critical to enrich our understanding of the nature of spiritual growth by exposing ourselves to feminist and other liberation theologians. The spiritual growth of many men and women is blocked by the fact that they experience spiritual realities screened through and limited by the patriarchial experience. A new flowering of spiritual life is now possible and is in fact occurring where people are open to the contribution of women and to the so-called feminine side of all persons and of divinity.

A New Day for Fathers

Abundant research findings make it clear that fathers as well as mothers are vital in the development of children as whole persons. The *de facto* consignment of so many fathers to the edge of the lives of their children has had many deleterious effects on children. The future wholeness of our children depends on our getting it together as men and women. One sex cannot be truly free unless the other is free.

The excitement of changing identities of women and men is in the awareness that we now have the possibility of nearly doubling the pool of leadership and creativity available to the human race, without adding to the population, by freeing women and men to use all of themselves. If the human family is to survive we will need all the creativity and leadership we can release.

As both men and women are freer to become fuller selves, according to their unique possibilities, not limited by set-in-concrete roles, unprecedented dimensions of creative fathering are developing.

The emerging new day for fathers poses a profound challenge—a challenge to move beyond obsolete ways of relating and to find more creative identities as men, husbands, fathers, and human beings. This makes the present a risky but exciting time for fathers.

As Myron Brenton puts the issue, "It simply requires a man to be more fully human, more responsive, and more fully functioning than he has ever before allowed himself to be. This is the freedom that equality of the sexes offers him." [14]

The challenge for both women and men is to create new ways of relating to each other and to children. In a real sense, this involves becoming new people. It is good news that the capacity for this newness is within us all.

Chapter VIII

Happiness Is a Warm Father: Some Characteristics and Implications of Liberated Fathering

Charlotte Holt Clinebell

> He too is a nice and gentle Person
> and has feelings like any Ordinary Person
> Do you like your Father? I do.
> *JoAnne*[1]

As I prepare to write an article about fathering, I am aware of many feelings about my own father. I wonder whether everyone who wrote a chapter for this anthology began with similar feelings. Perhaps behind the collection of words that now appear in print in this volume is a myriad of memories, thoughts, and feelings about the authors' own fathers, whether those fathers were emotionally or physically present or absent, whether the relationships were joyful or painful, affirming or rejecting, or some combination of all those things. Perhaps also the readers of these pages find their thoughts drifting to their experience of being or not being fathered. And perhaps those writers and readers who are themselves fathers, think about their sense of success and failure, joy and pain, around their own fathering. Whether they are good or bad, whether they are there or not there, in our culture fathers are important.

Warm memories of my father crowd around me as I write, especially from the early years. There were games of monopoly and crokinole on the living room floor; there were croquet games in the backyard and ball games with the neighborhood children; there were Sunday evenings in front of the fireplace—I can still hear the popcorn popping. I can still see, too, the playhouse my father built while I was in the hospital for a tonsillectomy and feel the joy I felt when I saw it waiting for me. I remember dark nights under the stars when I learned about the constellations and overcame the terrors of the night: "No, there's nothing scary behind that bush!" There are memories of bandaged knees and sympathy after I fell down, of mounds of dishes we washed together, of his dismantling the "day after" turkey and enjoying every minute of it, especially the bones! I remember the wooden seat fixed high in the walnut tree where I could sit and survey the neighborhood and dream. I remember my father's warmth and protectiveness toward my mother and his complete willingness to help with the housework and child care. And I felt safe with my father. One winter the creek near our house overflowed; I was frightened until I looked out and saw my father with the other neighborhood men digging channels and sandbagging our house. "It must be all right if Daddy is in charge!"

Of course, there is pain among my memories, too. My father didn't believe in anger or disobedience either, and there was a particular bush with long stems that made good switches when the leaves were removed. Oh, the humiliation! I remember, too, the sense of loss I felt as I grew older and my father seemed less available for good times. Now, as I look back, I realize that although he was much more involved with home and children than were most men, the demands of breadwinning and of succeeding in his profession made it progressively more difficult for him to stay close to his children. Most of the actual dirty work and discipline of raising us fell to my mother; she was the one I turned to both for comfort in times of hurt and with my anger and rebelliousness as I grew more independent. Most of my memories about my father are of fun together. He was the good guy. I never got to know his other side, or to know him well, as I did my mother.

Yes, my father was a nurturing person, but society did not make it easy or even possible for him to express that nurturance fully. Why should that be? It is still true now, forty years later, that we expect mothers to be closer to children than fathers. Within the last one hundred years, and particularly within the last fifty, the father who goes off to work and returns at the end of the day to be nurtured himself has become increasingly the normative image of fathering. The distant father—distant from the standpoint of direct physical care and close emotional ties—is a prevalent pattern in most cultures.

Has the patriarchal pattern, father as authority and mother as child nurturer, always been the norm? Is it changing? What would a society be like in which both parents were nurturers? Is there such a thing as the "maternal" instinct in men—or even in women?

Many people argue that because it has always been so (man the hunter, the strong one; woman the mother, the weak one) it must always remain so. The assumption (and sometimes fanatical conviction) that nurturing is learned behavior, not something that comes naturally, on the part of the male and innate, an instinct, on the part of the female has powerful evidence in its favor both in the animal and in the human world. In much of the animal world the male has nothing to do with the female and her offspring beyond

mating. Some primate males protect and provide for the
females and the young but do not nurture them directly. Of
course, there are exceptions. Some male animals and birds
feed their young; some male fish carry the eggs and hatch the
baby fish.

There are exceptions in the human world as well, but they
are exceptions. The obvious biological connection between
mother and child from conception to weaning and the fact
that most mothers in most societies appear to have felt a close
emotional physical and spiritual attachment to their children
makes it easy to assume some sort of instinct. It took a long
time, no one really knows how many hundreds of thousands
of years, for human beings to discover that males also create
children.

Matriarchy, or *mother right*, refers to societies in which
women had considerable prestige and power. Descent and
property usually passed through the female. There is no firm
data to indicate that these were and are societies in which
women were considered superior or dominant or held
physical power over men, although that remains open to
question. The earliest modern champion of mother right
remarked that "the father is always a juridical fiction, the
mother a physical fact."[2] People in at least one contemporary
human society—the Trobriand Islands—profess not to be
aware of the connection between intercourse and childbirth.[3]
And even in twentieth-century technological civilization,
specific paternity is impossible to prove. These facts
contribute to the apparent "naturalness" of the distant father
and the nurturing mother.

The myths of many cultures attest to the human awareness
that the fact of bearing and nurturing children separates
woman from man. In Maori myth

the Earth and Sky lay blended in the close embrace of
matrimony for an indefinite period. Children were born to

them in confined space. Light awaited the revolt of the brood which existed in darkness under the armpits of the Earth-Mother.

The children got tired of being so cramped and decided to separate their parents. One of them stood on tiptoe with arms stretched high and pushed the father into the sky where he remains to this day.

> The grief of Rangi [father] and Papa [mother] at their separation was intense. The tears of Rangi rained down in a continuous flood accompanied by hail and snow. From Papa rose perpetual mists, and the dampness of grief was congealed on her body into bitter frosts.[4]

It is the children who push their parents apart. They remain close to the mother while the father is relegated to outer space.

In human experience as well, the separation of woman from man accompanies the conception and birth of children. Campbell quotes an Abyssinian woman:

> How can a man know what a woman's life is? A woman's life is quite different from a man's. . . . A man is the same from the time of his circumcision to the time of his withering. . . . The man spends a night by a woman and goes away. His life and body are always the same. The woman conceives. As a mother she is another person than the woman without child. . . . Something grows into her life that never departs from it. . . . She is a mother. . . . And this the man does not know; he knows nothing. He does not know the difference before love and after love, before motherhood and after motherhood. . . . Only a woman can know that and speak of that.[5]

In our own society it is often true that the mother's close biological experience of carrying, bearing, and nurturing a child is one which shuts out the father. That may be particularly the case in cultures like ours that emphasize the man's world outside the home as the important one and encourage women to find their only or chief fulfillment in bearing and rearing children. Whether the time and place is matriarchal or patriarchal, most cultures that we know about assign childrearing to the female and keep the male busy hunting or fighting or building skyscrapers.

But is it either desirable or necessary that it always be so? Need the admittedly different biological experience of procreation separate women and men from one another and fathers from their children? Probably neither sex can fully understand the sexual and procreative adventure of the other. It is one thing to carry a growing life within one's body for nine months, deliver that life into the world in pain and ecstasy, and then feed that life from one's own breasts. Providing the other half of the seed, even in a moment of joy, and then being physically separate from the growing life must be a different emotional and physical and spiritual experience.

The difference, however, has had a variety of consequences. It hasn't always meant that men were the superior sex and that women raised the children. A growing body of literature in mythology, archaeology, anthropology, and prehistory suggests long millennia of prepatriarchal times when the Earth Mother, the Lady of the Wild Things, and then the Great Goddess of earliest agricultural times, was dominant.[6] Woman's clear connection with the cycle of birth and death meant that she enjoyed a great influence, prestige, and power. Her role as the creator of life endowed her with tremendous importance. That did not mean that men were necessarily secondary or powerless. Many such societies were apparently benevolent, peaceful, and egalitarian.[7] There are a few incompletely documented stories of Amazonian societies that suggest that there may have been prehistorical times and places where women did take political control and turn over the children they bore to male "mothers" to raise.[8]

After the advent of the Sky Father god and the decline of the Earth Mother goddess, the status and prestige of woman also decreased. She continued to be the child nurturer, but that role lost its status as men discovered their part in procreation and exercised their power. But even in modern patriarchal times when women are generally considered inferior and child nurturing is not the important work, there are variations on the traditional patriarchal themes. Among the Arapesh of New Guinea, women and men participate together in home life; men take as much care of children as do women; and, in a practice known as *couvade*, they participate in labor, delivery, and confinement when their children are born.[9] Ilongot males of the Phillipines share the housework and have close relationships with their children.[10] The Mbuti of Africa and the Trobriand Islanders are societies in which women and men cooperate in the home.[11] Some matrifocal societies, like the Javanese of Indonesia are reminiscent of earlier eras when motherhood was the important role and the father was an irrelevant item in the household.[12] And then there are the Mundugumor of New Guinea whose children are not particularly wanted or valued and neither women nor men want to take care of them.[13] Fathers in Trobriand Island society, where a father is merely "the husband of my mother," nevertheless care for and form close attachments to their children.[14] Societies in which child-rearing is valued as the important work, in which nurturing is considered a male prerogative, in which parenting is shared, in which the sexes are equally valued, though rare, are nevertheless within the range of human experience. Contemporary American society, with its growing emphasis on the importance and value of fathering, may be helping us toward a new era, neither matriarchal nor patriarchal, in which women and men share the important tasks and satisfactions of life, both domestic and social.

The new awareness of and interest in the importance of fathering has probably been kindled by the growth of the women's liberation movement. Many women have become aware that they have been getting most of the burden of raising children and little of the satisfaction of developing other interests and talents. They have discovered that as a result, much of the joy of bearing and raising children has vanished. Women have begun to call for shared parenting, public child care, increased opportunities outside the home. A recent Roper poll, which interviewed three thousand women, found that "61 percent of all women under thirty favor a marriage of equal partnership, where husband and wife both work and share homemaking and child-care responsibilities."[15] These new demands dovetail with what psychologists and sociologists in American society have been saying for some time—that children get too much mother and not enough father and that such a situation can be destructive. More than the question of women's rights is at stake, although that is a vital issue. Numerous studies document the deleterious effects on children of absent or distant fathers and hovering mothers, an inevitable combination in a culture that defines woman's success by the success of her children and man's success by the money or prestige he acquires.[16]

Fortunately, there seems to be a growing interest among men in the rights and responsibilities and joys and pain of fathering. While women have begun to redefine themselves as strong and competent as well as tender and nurturing, men have begun to discover their gentle and caring capacities. A spate of recent books and articles describes the new experience and feelings of some men as they move into

the world of women.[17] One father remarked, when he
stopped being a visitor in his own home,

> I heard and saw firsthand the brilliant and ingenious things all
> babies do for their mothers and that their mothers explain to
> their fathers when they come home from work. I was there, I
> was part of it—the teething, the first steps, the visits to the
> pediatrician.[18]

Another father who has full responsibility for his children
says:

> Being a parent has helped me learn about me, helped me realize
> how little I understood about women before, helped me
> discover the children as people, and helped them really know
> me.[19]

One father feels both the joy and the pain:

> There is a wondrous security in feeding a baby his bottle
> (providing it is not four A.M.) that we men are discovering now
> that you women have jumped the fence and are tasting the
> grass in more distant fields.[20]

Of course, it isn't all easy; it means sharing the hard parts
(including the 4 A.M. feedings) and the dirty work as well as
the fun. A graduate student says:

> We're both much more tired at the end of a day than we used to
> be. . . . Whenever we talk about having another child, we
> think about the fatigue and then we think about the enriched
> good feelings and that makes the hassle melt away. . . . Sure
> it's a role conflict to give time to Cedar rather than to my
> work—and it's taking me one-third longer to complete my
> master's program. Many people don't understand me when I
> say I can't participate in a seminar because I want to be home to
> take care of my son.[21]

Many fathers are now becoming involved with their
children during pregnancy and childbirth. Like the Arapesh,

they "give birth to" and "grow" their babies along with the mother. Parents take classes together before the birth, exercise together, and the father learns how to work with the mother through labor right up to delivery; very often the father is the one to lay the baby on the mother's breast. Though the experience is obviously very different for each parent, the father's sense of involvement throughout pregnancy and the birth is the beginning of shared parenting. One father described it thus: "It was the most incredible, wonderful, terrifically joyful, sexual, sensual, loving time of our lives. . . . It was extraordinary for us because we did it together."[22] The father I have known best, other than my own father, is the father of my children. Howard says that as he has in recent years felt more responsibility for our children, taken a greater interest in their development, and spent more time with them, he also feels much closer to them. And as he has moved closer to them, I have been able to let go of some of my overbearing and overprotective mothering, which was bad for them and for me too.

Unfortunately, not all fathers feel the need to be closer to their children, nor do they understand the needs of the children and the mothers for a fairer sharing of the parent responsibility. The little book called *What is a Father? Children's Responses*, which is quoted at the beginning of this chapter, contains some warm responses like JoAnne's but also some sad ones. Many fathers still remain distant, sometimes by choice or because of their image of what a father should be, sometimes because of the demands of a job and financial responsibility for the family. The awesome children feel for their fathers is illustrated in the following comments from that little book:

He is always bursting with advices. *Willie*

A father in my opinion is one who more or less sets an example. *Pete*

> A father is someone to be respected. He sometimes takes the
> place of God. *Albert*

And there is a good deal of wisdom in the following
comment:

> Daddys were put on the earth for the purpose to take care of us
> kids. And some do and some don't. *Dave*

It's interesting that the above are all the remarks of little
boys. Like JoAnne, girls seem to make more positive remarks
about fathers:

> A father is a man who picks you up and holds you tight when
> you are little and afraid. *Maureen*

> What a father is? He does not love you because your pretty or
> tall or small. He loves you because your you. God bless my
> father. *Margaret*

It is certainly true that fathers treat sons and daughters
differently (so do mothers). Fathers tend to be more
demanding and emotionally distant with sons and more
affectionate and protective with daughters. Because fathers
(and mothers too) treat boys and girls so differently, neither
sex gets a balanced picture of what it means to develop one's
full personality. There seem to me to be two characteristics of
a liberated or whole person.[23] (Not that anyone ever really
arrives at complete liberation or wholeness. It is a process not
a finality.) One is an *independent sense of self* and the other is
a *capacity for intimate relationships.* Unfortunately we have all
too often assigned each of these characteristics to a different
sex. Boys often become so independent that they think they
don't or shouldn't need to depend on others. They grow up
believing that intimacy or closeness is "feminine" and
therefore a sign of weakness. Girls, on the other hand,
develop the need and capacity for relationships, but often

they become so dependent on them that they have difficulty functioning alone. They do not develop an independent sense of self. Hence the need for a "derivative identity," usually through a man. Why not encourage both autonomy and interdependence in both girls and boys?

We seem also to find it easier to allow girls to move into traditionally male areas than to allow boys to move into traditionally female ones. Perhaps that is because we value men more than women? When girls and women adopt traditionally female behavior, they are becoming "weaker." Girls can be tomboys, but boys cannot be sissies. Girls can wear pants, but boys can't wear dresses. We worry more about boys playing with dolls than we do about girls playing with trucks. Girls becoming part of organizations like Little League threatens people not so much because the girls will be hurt as because the male world is being invaded and may be weakened or destroyed. Studies both formal and informal document the difficulties both sexes have in letting men and boys express their soft, tender, gentle, nurturing, and vulnerable sides. A recent series of interviews with a group of avowed feminist mothers of sons indicated that even these "liberated" women felt at best ambivalent about their relationships with their sons and at worst powerless to prevent them from growing up into male chauvinists. Most of these mothers were reluctant to encourage in their sons the kind of "other sex" behavior they felt free to encourage in their daughters.[24]

Children learn very early what our culture deems appropriate for men and fathers. *William's Doll* is the story of a little boy who wants a doll more than anything.[25] His brother and his friend and his father all laugh at him and his father gives him a train set and a basketball in order to distract him. He likes those things but he is not distracted. Then grand-mother, recognizing the wisdom of William's desire, buys him a doll. When father protests she explains herself by saying that he needs it to love and to diaper and to "bring up a bubble" so he can practice being a father. A teacher in New York asked her fourth-, fifth-, and sixth-grade students what they thought of the story. The comments were many and varied. Here are a few.

> I don't think a boy should have a doll because it can send him on the wrong road to be a man.

> Ladies are doctors, and men are nurses. Fully grown boys have ladies purses. Then why can't boys have dolls for their toys?

> I think it was a very dumb idea about William buying a doll. A father shouldn't have to take care of a baby. A mother should. I think William is a *Sissy*. *Sissy* and a *queer*.

> I think a boy should have a doll. A doll gives security and he learns to love and care for his own child. It may sound silly, but I think that's the most wonderful thing a boy can have.[26]

We will not grow warm and liberated fathers until we free little boys to develop their soft and tender and nurturing sides.

The title of this chapter suggests some connection between a warm father and liberated fathering. Of course, there have always been warm fathers, fathers who felt both close to and responsible for the full care of their children. But our institutions and attitudes continue to make things difficult for such fathers. Are we ready for a new definition of liberated fathering, one that brings fathers closer to mothers and to children and that frees mothers and children and fathers, too, to develop their own full humanness? Such a definition of liberated fathering is not really different from one of liberated mothering or parenting. It is related to the demands of women for equality and for shared parenting. It is related to the rights of children to have warm loving relationships with adults of both sexes and to develop their full personalities. It is also related to the fact that children can now be chosen, that marriage without children is now a satisfying option, that people can choose to have children for new reasons, that life can be full and satisfying for either men or women without one's own children as well as with them. Such a definition must be based on the assumption that both sexes are important, not one more than the other, and that "the most important work in the world is the participation in the care and growth of human life."[27] If I were asked to define for contemporary American society a liberated father or liberated fathering, I would say that a liberated father is one who finds as much satisfaction in relationships with his children and takes as much responsibility for their physical and emotional care as he does in and for his job, career, or other activities. The implications of such a definition for our culture are as profound and widespread as those of the emancipation and full equality of women. For such a concept to become actual practice, we would have to let go of the belief that a male person is superior to a female one. We would have to view a man not simply as success and power-oriented but as the nice and gentle person with feelings like anybody else described by JoAnne at the outset of this chapter. Perhaps her definition is the best.

If such a view of fathering were to become generally accepted, it would mean major changes in the way we relate to one another as women and men in both private and public life. Marriages and families would be different, schools and churches would be different, business and industry and government would be different. It's hard to imagine what it would be like if women and men shared equally in home and public life, but maybe a few speculations are possible. What we're talking about is a basic change in our value system.

If men were as interested in the nurturing of human growth as they are in other aspects of their lives, they would demand an equal share in the parenting of children. They would insist on the chance to stay home more. That would mean that women would have to "move over"—they would have to be willing to share the satisfactions as well as the burdens of parenting with fathers. If men were to have their full share of the parenting, women would have to take more responsibility in the world outside the home—more responsibility for earning money, more responsibility for shaping and administering public policy. Women already comprise more than one third of the work force, mostly in low-paying, low-prestige jobs. If they were to insist on men sharing the work of the home to the extent that women do the menial jobs in industries and offices, all the institutions of society—government, business, industry, education, the church—would have to provide the kind of environment that would allow both parents to be with children. That might mean a variety of arrangements—part-time days, weeks, years; paternity as well as maternity leaves. It would mean that hospitals would provide facilities for fathers to participate in labor and childbirth and to be with child and mother during the first days after birth. Or maybe childbirth would return to the home; it already has in some places.

The change in our value structure that would be heralded by such a change in the attitude of men toward childbirth and childrearing would mean that fathers (as well as mothers) would present a new model of human wholeness to their children. Both boys and girls would value tenderness, nurturing, and compassion. Both girls and boys would value assertiveness and independence. We would develop a new definition of success and achievement. Fathers (and mothers) would encourage their daughters as well as their sons to explore career options from medicine to politics. Fathers (and mothers) would encourage their sons as well as their daughters to care for children, to cook and sew and type. Both boys and girls would view the possibility of parenting as one option among many. The focus would be on individual interests and talents instead of on sex-role stereotypes. Whether or not people chose to become parents, what creative and career interests they chose would depend on individual differences not on sex.

In a world that needs to control rather than expand population growth, smaller families for people who want to raise children would be necessary and important. Or maybe couples who find great satisfaction in the nurturing of children would have larger families while other people did other kinds of work. Public policy would subsidize such families. In a society which encouraged both women and men to develop their nurturing capacities, people who chose not to have children of their own would find nurturing opportunities available in all the human services. If nurturing were truly valued as much as material success and status, people would put far greater energies into eradicating poverty, feeding the world, bringing peace.

In such a society, men would choose to have children for different reasons than they now do. Instead of wanting sons to perpetuate their names and daughters to possess and protect, in a nonpatriarchal society both men and women, if they choose to have children, would do so because they like them, because they love life and want to pass it on, because they want the enrichment that participating in the growth of children can bring. Daughters and sons would be equally valued; the child would count more than its sex.

Such a society sounds idealistic. Certainly we are a long way from the reality of it. But as women ask for more help with parenting and more men respond to the cry, significant challenges to public policy are beginning to be made. Not only are the rights of mothers being noticed, but also the rights of fathers. One school-teaching father in New York applied for "paternity leave and child care" on the same basis as maternity leave is granted to women—leave of absence without pay or part-time work for up to seven years. But he was denied the same treatment. He wanted to do substitute teaching on a part-time basis so that he could be with his child while she was small. He is still fighting the discriminatory decision (with the help of the ACLU) because he believes that the rights of fathers and of children are at stake.[28] Gradual changes in public policy that give fathers equal rights to child care and child custody will result if fathers continue to recognize the value for themselves and their children of their getting more involved in home and family life.

The question of whether men and fathers will ever really share equally in home and child care is probably closely bound to the strength of women's demands for liberation. It is unlikely that most men will be willing to take the risks of becoming more responsible for the nurturing care of children and the home unless and until women refuse to accept the old way any more. And it may also be true that fathers will not discover the joys of closer involvement with their children until they've tried it awhile. Fathers and mothers, women and men, can help each other to learn how to balance the instrumental and the expressive capacities that we have traditionally divided between the sexes. The one great danger of the women's liberation movement is that women will forget the values of closeness and compassion, nurturing and giving, as they move toward equality in a male world. Equality we must have, but that must not mean that women simply become like men; increasingly, we must challenge and change a society that places its greatest value on competitiveness, material success, status, and power. At its best, women's liberation will provide the impetus for developing a more humanizing society that draws on the best of both worlds—the traditionally "feminine" and the traditionally "masculine"—and makes possible greater individual and collective wholeness. If men in any numbers begin to realize that men's liberation means learning to nurture and to affirm the tender side, the impetus toward a more benevolent society will increase.

There is some evidence that when men are closely involved in home and child care, a more peaceable and egalitarian society results. When the assymetry of the sexes and of domestic and political life are minimized, so are violence, war, fear, suspicion, inequality. Relatively egalitarian societies such as the Ilongot of the Phillipines, the Mbuti of Africa, the Arapesh of New Guinea, the Andaman Islanders of the Bay of Bengal, and the Tasaday of the Phillipines, in which women and men share the work of the home and of the community, are relatively harmonious, amicable, and benevolent.[29] Of course, we cannot expect, nor do we desire, to model our society in any concrete ways after these less sophisticated cultures. But we could and perhaps *must* learn from them both the possibilities and importance of reducing the antagonism between the sexes and between the domestic and public spheres of our society.

Some research closer to home suggests that our survival may lie in a new direction for human society. Sandra Bem, a psychologist at Stanford University has developed an androgyny scale.[30] She defines an androgynous person as one who has the capacity to behave appropriately as the situation requires—to be gentle when gentleness is needed, to be decisive when that is crucial. She finds that those men and women who are either "strongly masculine" or "strongly feminine" have limited or crippled personalities, that is, they cannot respond as the situation dictates. In Bem's experiments such individuals had trouble either playing with a kitten or exhibiting independence in deciding which cartoons were funny or both. Androgynous persons could do either. They were also found to be more creative, more intelligent, and more tolerant than those individuals who were limited to sex stereotypical behavior. Her findings suggest, as do the examples of the relatively egalitarian societies mentioned above, that psychic or psychological or spiritual wholeness, individually and collectively, is closely related to the degree of symmetry of sex roles. It may be that a post-matriarchal and post-patriarchal society will see the development of an androgynous or gynandrous consciousness, one in which an individual and collective psychological and spiritual wholeness is present. That would simply mean that individuals were free to engage in activities and express feelings according to individual endowment and interest and that public policy would support such a standard of humanness.

We have come to a time in human history when we need to "combine political goals with utopian visions."[31] One vital aspect of such an effort is the need for men and fathers to participate fully in domestic life and for women to participate fully in public life.

The father's current abandonment of the mother and the child in the process of child rearing is a characteristic of our society so accepted that we hardly recognize its destructiveness. Instead of saying that men must do the important work and make the important decisions, while women raise the children, we might say that the most important work in the world is the participation in the care and growth of human life. We might provide first for women and men to develop as individuals and relate as equals and then to share equally in the important work of child rearing if they choose to do so. . . . The child is led to believe that he or she has a father, and in essence, he or she does *not*. Rather, the child has a legal relative who says, in effect, "I am dominant and do the important things. I leave the major interaction in your development to your mother because it is a lesser matter." The inevitable conclusion is that dominance and important affairs do not include involvement in the growth of another human being. . . . Here is a whole new realm of living from which traditional values have excluded men and in which they might find one source of the human connection and engagement that many seek desperately today.[32]

Earlier I raised some questions about the maternal instinct. Of course, I have not answered them. We know little yet about what is innate and what is acquired, especially in the area of sex differences.[33] But it does seem clear, to me at least, that the maternal instinct is a concept that grew out of the biological fact that women until now have spent most of their adult lives bearing and raising children, while men were first hunters and finally technologists. Now women are no longer confined to childbirth and home, and hunters are obsolete. Technology means that there is almost no kind of work that can't be done by either sex. Some women aren't interested in nurturing children. Lots of men are.

So perhaps we must replace the concept of the maternal instinct with that of the nurturing instinct, or at least, the nurturing capacity. The capacity for nurturing and enjoying it appears to be a human one rather than sex specific. We now know that fathers can be good "mothers" and that mothers can be good "fathers." Both can love and care, earn money, set a good example, give advice, and command respect. Shared parenting demands that both parents be able and willing to wash the diapers, prepare the food, pay the bills, supply the sympathy and understanding, set the limits and standards, and challenge and encourage the fullest development of all aspects of the child's personality. One father describes it thus:

The real authority figure in our house is a two-headed entity, Mommy-and-Daddy, which I suppose makes me only half a paterfamilias. Some might find this arrangement threatening or cumbersome; it strikes me as eminently practical.[34]

As is always true of something new, it will be harder and maybe more confusing for parents to learn to share the task of childrearing in new ways. Old role divisions were easy to understand if not to follow. As parents experiment with new ways there will be lots of new decisions to make; in the transition, parents and children may be uncertain. But if a father and a mother are committed to each other's growth and development as well as to their children's growth, they will be able to work out a creative style that fits their own needs and circumstances.

As our society continues to broaden its acceptance (if it does) of a variety of life-styles, the possibilities for creative parenting boggle the mind! We know from our own and other cultures that children thrive in many different milieux—the nuclear family isn't the only one and maybe isn't the best. We're becoming aware that children need more than one adult of each sex both as role models and as loving, caring human beings on whom they can depend. The extended family system, prevalent in many cultures and in former times in our own, provides the security of a number of loving adults. Children in the Andaman Islands are often adopted by several sets of parents in succession. In our own society there are many successful solo parents of both sexes; they are most apt to raise free children if they can provide other adult relationships of warmth and caring as well as their own. It is interesting that concomitant with the increased involvement of fathers at home and mothers outside the home, public policy has begun to affirm solo parenting. Several states now allow the adoption of children by single women and men. More and more nonmarried mothers are keeping their babies. We now need also to provide a supportive environment of other adults of both sexes for such parents and children. It seems likely that we will discover that many styles of parenting are creative, from communes and kibbutzes to the nuclear family, once the nurturing of human life becomes individually and collectively valued as the most important work in the world.

We are only beginning to get the distant Sky Father back down from the sky. Perhaps that has implications for our concept of a Father God in heaven—far away, judging, powerful. A Mother–Father God would be closer, more nurturing, more affirming of our wholeness as part of the ecology of the universe. An androgynous or gynandrous God may become part of the new era into which we move as we give up the excesses of patriarchal society and adopt a system that is committed to the fullest possible flowering of every person. Creative fathering in such a society must go hand in hand with the rights of children, of women, and of men to food; health and shelter; emotional, mental, and spiritual wholeness.

An ancient Chinese scripture says, "From wonder into wonder, existence opens." Or as a school child wrote after studying about airplanes: "Many of the things about airplanes that were once thought to be science fiction now actually are. From now on, I will put both gladness and wonder in my same thought about airplanes."[35] And I will do the same about fathers. Happiness *is* a warm, caring, struggling, nurturing, succeeding and failing, hurting and rejoicing father.

Notes

CHAPTER 1

1. Urie Bronfenbrenner, "The Changing American Child," *Journal of Social Issues*, 17 (1961), 6-18.

2. Urie Bronfenbrenner, *Two Worlds of Childhood: U.S. and U.S.S.R.* (New York: Russell Sage Foundation, 1970), p. 104.

3. Related in a symposium on homosexuality at the Annual Meeting of the American Association of Pastoral Counselors, San Francisco, California, November, 1971. For further writing on this subject by Dr. Bieber, see Alfred M. Freedman and H. I. Kaplan, *Comprehensive Textbook of Psychiatry* (Baltimore: Williams & Wilkins, 1967).

4. Fritz Redl and David Wineman, *The Aggressive Child* (New York: The Free Press, 1957), p. 203.

5. Hans Kummer, *Primate Societies* (Chicago: Oldine, Atherton, 1971), p. 150.

6. *Ibid.*, p. 34.

7. Sigmund Freud, *The Ego and the Id* (London: Hogarth Press, 1927), p. 39.

8. David P. Ausubel, *Ego Development and the Personality Disorders* (New York: Grune & Stratton, 1952).

9. Leighton McCutchen, "The Father Figure in Psychology and Religion," *Journal of the American Academy of Religion*, 40 (1972), 176.

10. Erich Neumann, *The Origins and History of Consciousness*, 2 vols. (New York: Harper & Brothers, 1962).

11. Erik H. Erikson, *Identity and the Life Cycle* (New York: International Universities Press, 1959), p. 141.

12. Robert Lifton, "Protean Man" (Address delivered at the Conference on Studies of the Acquisition and Development of Values, Washington, D.C., May 15-17, 1968).

13. Alexander Mittscherlich, *Society Without the Father: A Contribution to Social Psychology* (New York: Harcourt Brace Jovanovich, 1963), p. 218.

14. McCutchen, "Father Figure," p. 176.

15. *Ibid.*, p. 176.

16. *Ibid.*, p. 176.

CHAPTER 2

1. Victor White, *God and the Unconscious,* (London: Harvill Press, 1952).

CHAPTER 3

1. C. G. Jung, "A Psychological Approach to the Trinity," *Psychology and Religion: West and East* (Princeton: Princeton University Press, 1958), pp. 130, 149 n. *Psychology and Religion* is vol. 11 in *The Collected Works of C. G. Jung*, translated by R. F. C. Hull and published by the Bollingen Foundation. *The Collected Works* will hereafter be referred to as CW.

2. Jung, *Aion* (CW vol. 9, part 2, 1959), p. 18; see also Jung, *Symbols of Transformation* (CW 5, 1967), p. 44n.

3. Jung, *Psychology and Religion*, pp. 132-33.

4. C. G. Jung, *Symbols of Transformation* (Princeton: Princeton University Press, 1976), I; see also Erich Neumann, *The Child*, trans. R. Manheim (New York: G. P. Putnam's Sons, 1973), pp. 189, 197.

5. Jung, *Psychology and Alchemy* (CW 12, 1953), p. 68.

6. Jung, *Aion*, p. 193; see also *Psychology and Religion*, p. 264.

7. Jung, *Mysterium Conjunctionis* (CW 14, 1963), p. 357.

8. Jung, *Psychology and Alchemy*, p. 62.

9. Neumann, *The Child*, p. 173.

10. *Ibid.*, p. 189.

11. *Ibid.*, p. 187.

12. Jung, *Psychology and Religion*, p. 176.

13. Ann B. Ulanov, *The Feminine in Jungian Psychology and in Christian Theology*, (Evanston, Ill.: Northwestern University Press, 1971).

CHAPTER 4

1. John Bowlby, "The Influence of Early Environment in the Development of Neurosis and Neurotic Character," *International Journal of Psychoanalysis*, 21 (1940), 154-78; Bowlby, *Maternal Care and Mental Health*, World Health Organization, Monograph Series, no. 2 (Geneva, 1951); Bowlby, "Grief and Mourning in Infancy and Early Childhood," *The Psychoanalytic Study of the Child*, 15 (1960), 9-52; Bowlby, *Attachment and Loss*, 2 vols. (New York: Basic Books, 1973), 1 *Attachment*, 2 *Separation*.

2. Rene A. Spitz, "Hospitalization: An Inquiry into the Genesis of Psychiatric Conditions in Early Childhood," *The Psychoanalytic Study of the Child*, 1 (1945), 53-74; Spitz, "Anaclitic Depression: An Inquiry into the Genesis of Psychiatric Conditions in Early Childhood," *Psychoanalytic Study of Child*, 2 (1946), 313-42.

3. Anna Freud and Dorothy T. Burlingham, *War and Children* (New York: Ernest Willard, 1943); Freud, "About Losing and Being Lost," *The Psychoanalytic Study of the Child*, 22 (1967), 9-19.

4. T. Holmes, in Alvin Toffler, *Future Shock* (New York, Random House, 1970), p. 329.

5. K. R. Eissler, "Death Drive, Ambivalence, and Narcissism," *The Psychoanalytic Study of the Child*, 26 (1971), 25-78; Erik Erikson, *Childhood and*

Society (New York: W. W. Norton and Co., 1950); Erikson, "Identity and the Lifecycle," *Psychological Issues* (New York: International Universities Press, 1950); M. S. Mahler, "On Sadness and Grief in Infancy and Childhood: Loss and Restoration of the Symbolic Love Object," *Psychoanalytic Study of Child*, 16 (1961), 332-51; H. Nagera, "Children's Reactions to the Death of Important Objects: A Developmental Approach," *Psychoanalytic Study of Child*, 25 (1970), 360-400; P. B. Neubauer, "The One-Parent Child and His Oedipal Development," *Psychoanalytic Study of Child*, 15 (1960), 286-309; C. J. Newman, "Children of Disaster: Clinical Observations at Buffalo Creek," *American Journal of Psychiatry*, 133 (March, 1976), 306-12; G. Rochlin, "Loss and Restitution," *Psychoanalytic Study of Child*, 8 (1953), 288-309; A. E. Scharl, "Regression and Restitution in Object Loss: Clinical Observations," *Psychoanalytic Study of Child*, 16 (1961), 471-80.

6. C. Wahl, "The Fear of Death," *Bulletin of the Menninger Clinic*, 22 (1958), 214-23, in Herman Feifel, ed., *The Meaning of Death*. (New York, McGraw-Hill Book Co., 1959).

7. Harry F. Harlow and Margaret K. Harlow, "Social Deprivation in Monkeys," *Scientific American*, 207 (November, 1962), 136-46.

8. Henry B. Biller, "Father Absence and the Personality Development of the Male Child," *Annual Progress in Child Psychiatry and Child Development*, ed. Stella Chess and Alexander Thomas, 7 vols. (New York: Brunner-Mazel, 1971) 4, 120-52; J. Louis Despert, *Children of Divorce* (Garden City, N.Y.: Doubleday & Co., 1962); J. B. McDermott, "Divorce and its Psychiatric Sequelae in Children," *Archives of General Psychiatry*, 23 (1970), 421-27.

9. T. L. Trunnell, "The Absent Fathers: Children's Emotional Disturbances," *Archives of General Psychiatry*, 19 (August, 1968), 641-49.

10. H. L. Wylie and R. A. Delgado, "A Pattern of Mother-Son Relationships Involving the Absence of Father," *American Journal of Orthopsychiatry*, 29 (1959), 644-49.

11. M. L. Meiss, "The Oedipal Problem of a Fatherless Child" *The Psychoanalytical Study of the Child*, (1952), pp. 216-29.

12. Anonymous, "Letter to Dad from a Doctor's Daughter," *Physician's Management*, October, 1975, pp. 25-27.

13. J. L. Kogelschatz, P. L. Adams, and D. M. Tucker, "Family Styles of Fatherless Households," *Journal of the American Academy of Child Psychiatry*, 1972, pp. 365-83.

14. Erna Furman, *A Child's Parent Dies* (New Haven: Yale University Press, 1974).

15. S. L. Baker, E. G. Fischer, L. A. Cove *et al.*, "Problems of Family Reintegration Following Prolonged Father Absence" (abstract), *Orthopsychiatry*, 38 (1968), 347; F. A. Pederson, "Relationship Between Father Absence and Emotional Disturbance in Male Military Dependents," *Merrill-Palmer Quarterly*, 12 (1966), 321-31.

16. Earl Lindemann, "The Symptomatology and Management of Acute Grief," *Death and Identity*, ed. Robert Fulton.

17. W. Lamers, "Death, Grief, Mourning, the Funeral and the Child" (Milwaukee: Bulfin Printers, 1965).

18. Frank Crumley and Ronald S. Blumenthal, "Children's Reactions to Temporary Loss of the Father," *The American Journal of Psychiatry*, 130 (July, 1973), 778-82; W. J. Dickerson, R. J. Arthur, "Navy Families in Distress," *Military Medicine*, 130 (1965), 894-98; G. Gabower, "Problems of Childen in Navy Officers' Families," *Social Casework*, 41 (1960), 177-84; J. A. Kenny, "The Child in the Military Community," *Journal of the American Academy of Child Psychiatry*, 6 (1967), 51-53.

19. J. Hilgard and M. Newman, "Parental Loss by Death in Childhood as an Etiological Factor Among Schizophrenics and Adult Alcoholic Patients, Compared with a Non-patient Community Sample," *Journal of Nervous and Mental Diseases*, 137 (July, 1963), 14-28.

20. Toffler, Future Shock, p. 329.

21. M. Ruben, "Delinquency: A Defense Against Loss of Objects and Reality," *The Psychoanalytic Study of the Child*.

22. Ian Gregory, "Retrospective Estimates of Orphanhood from Generational Life Tables," *Millbank Memorial Fund Quarterly*, July, 1965.

23. "Rising Problems of Single Parents," *U.S. News*, 75 (July 16, 1963), 32-35.

24. "More Women Head U.S. Homes," *U.S. News*, 77 (December 2, 1964), 85.

CHAPTER 5

1. "A Memory of Youth," *The Collected Poems of W. B. Yeats*, 2d ed. rev. (New York: The Macmillan Co., 1950), p. 121.

2. Yeats, *Collected Poems*, pp. 8-9.

3. Sigmund Freud, "Mourning and Melancholia," *A General Selection from the Works of Sigmund Freud* (London: Hogarth Press, 1973). A good description of reactive and psychotic depression can be found in Norman Cameron, *Personality Development and Psychopathy: A Dynamic Approach* (Boston: Houghton Mifflin, 1963).

4. Freud, "Mourning and Melancholia," pp. 412-42, 516-57.

5. Ruth L. Munroe, *Schools of Psychoanalytic Thought* (New York: Holt, Rinehart and Winston, 1955), pp. 357-58.

6. *Ibid.*, p. 359.

7. Otto Fenichel, *The Psychoanalytic Theory of Neurosis* (New York: W. W. Norton & Co., 1945), pp. 221, 224.

8. Kurt Koffka, *Principles of Gestalt Psychology* (New York: Harcourt Brace Jovanovich, 1935).

9. Carl Rogers, *Client Centered Therapy* (Boston: Houghton Mifflin, 1951), p. 486.

10. *Ibid.*, pp. 520-22.

11. Colin Murray Parkes, *Bereavement: Studies of Grief in Adult Life* (New York: International University Press, 1972).

12. Mwalimu Imara, "Dying as the Last Stage of Growth," in *Death As the Final Stage of Growth* (Englewood Cliffs, N.J.: Prentice-Hall, 1975), pp. 43, 55-77, 89-105.

13. Freud, "Mourning and Melancholia," p. 155.

14. Cameron, *Personality Development*, p. 436.

15. Imara, *Death as the Final Stage*, p. 436.

16. *Ibid.*, p. 155.

17. *Ibid.*, p. 161.

18. Ernest Becker, *The Denial of Death* (New York: The Free Press, 1973), p. 55.

CHAPTER 6

1. For example see H. B. Biller, *Paternal Deprivation* (Lexington, Mass.: Lexington Books, D.C. Heath, 1971); see also Alexander Mitscherlich, *Society Without the Father* (New York: Schocken Books, 1970).

2. Henry Biller and Dennis Meredith, *Father Power* (Anchor Books: Garden City N.Y.: Doubleday & Co., 1975), p. 7.

3. *Ibid.*, p. 355.

4. *Ibid.*, p. 356-57.

5. Ralph R. Greenson, *The Technique and Practice of Psychoanalysis* (New York: International Universities Press, 1967) I, 406.

6. *Ibid.*, pp. 185-87.

7. *Ibid.*, p. 187.

8. Jacqui Schiff, *All My Children* (Philadelphia: M. Evans, 1970), pp. 42-43.

9. *Ibid.*, p. 9.

10. *Ibid.*, p. 26.

11. *Ibid.*, p. 125.

12. Russell E. Osnes, "Spot Reparenting," *Transactional Analysis Journal*, 4, (July, 1974), 40-46.

13. *Ibid.*, p. 41.

14. *Ibid.*, p. 42.

15. *Ibid.*, pp. 43-44.

16. Quoted in Rogers, *Client Centered Therapy*, pp. 198-99.

17. *Ibid.*, p. 200.

18. *Ibid.*, pp. 28, 152.

19. David Ryback, review of *Fritz: An Intimate Portrait of Fritz Perls and Gestalt Therapy* by Martin Shepard, *Psychology Today*, 9 (September, 1975), 75.

20. Eric Berne, *Transactional Analysis in Psychotherapy* (New York: Grove Press, 1961), p. 161.

21. Greenson, *Technique and Practice*, p. 348.

22. John E. Mack and Elvin V. Semard, "Classical Psychoanalysis," *Comprehensive Textbook of Psychiatry* (Baltimore: Williams and Williams, 1967), p. 273.

23. Phyllis Chesler, *Women and Madness* (New York: Avon Books, 1972).

24. Women in Transition, Inc., *Women in Transition: A Feminist Handbook on Separation and Divorce* (New York: Charles Scribner's Sons, 1975), p. 404.

25. *Ibid.*, p. 462.

26. *Ibid.*, p. 463.

27. Chesler, *Women and Madness*, pp. 20, 138-39.

28. *Ibid.*, p. 139.

29. *Ibid.*, p. 143.

30. Maitland Zane, "Therapist Slept with Patients," *San Francisco Chronicle*, October 15, 1975, p. 2.

31. Biller and Meredith, *Father Power*, pp. 130, 135.

32. Chesler, *Women and Madness*, p. 138.

33. Talcott Parsons, *Social Structure and Personality* (New York: The Free Press, 1964), p. 67.

34. Chesler, *Women and Madness*, pp. 18-20.

35. Greenson, *Technique and Practice*, p. 238.

36. *Ibid.*, pp. 239, 240.

37. Nichols, Jack, *Male Liberation* (Baltimore: Penguin Books, 1975), p. 270.

38. Biller and Meredith, *Father Power*, p. 7.

39. Erica Jong, *Fear of Flying* (New York: New American Library, 1973), pp. 18-20.

40. *Ibid.*, pp. 310-11.

41. Jay Haley, *Strategies of Psychotherapy* (New York: Grune and Stratton, 1963), p. 193.

42. Sheldon B. Kopp, *If You Meet the Buddha on the Road, Kill Him!* (Palo Alto: Science and Behavior Books, 1972), pp. 41, 45.

43. Virginia Satir, *Peoplemaking* (Palo Alto: Science and Behavior Books, 1972).

44. Kopp, *If You Meet the Buddha*, p. 140.

CHAPTER 7

1. Myron Brenton, *The American Male, A Penetrating Look at the Masculinity Crisis* (New York: Coward, McCann, & Geoghegan, 1966), pp. 126-28.

2. David B. Lynn, *The Father: His Role in Child Development* (Monterey, Calif.: Brooks/Cole Publishing Co., 1974), pp. 226-27.

3. John Leonard, "Fathering Instinct," *Ms.*, 2 (May, 1974), 112.

4. *Ibid.*, p. 239.

5. *Ibid.*, pp. 172, 188, 214, 215. See also Brenton, *The American Male*, p. 7.

6. Charlotte H. Clinebell discusses the male box insightfully in *Meet Me in the Middle: How to Become Human Together* (New York: Harper & Row, 1973), chap. 2.

7. See my book, *The People Dynamic* (New York: Harper & Row, 1973), for

a discussion of how to set up a growth group; see also *Ms.* for suggestions on forming men's CR groups.

8. Howard J. Clinebell, *Growth Counseling for Marriage Enrichment: Pre-Marriage and the Early Years* (Philadelphia: Fortress Press, 1975), chap. 2.

9. See Arlo D. Compaan, "A Study of Contemporary Young Adult Marital Styles" (Th.D. diss., School of Theology, Claremont, 1973).

10. Henry B. Biller, *Father, Child and Sex Role* (Lexington, Mass.: Heath & Co., 1971) pp. 1-34; Henry B. Biller, *Parental Deprivation, Family, School, Sexuality and Society* (Heath & Co., 1974); E. Mavis Hetherington, "Girls Without Fathers," *Psychology Today*, February, 1973, pp. 47-52.

11. The Reverend Margaret Sawin of Rochester, New York, has developed this plan.

12. See Clinebell, *Growth Counseling for Marriage Enrichment.*

13. Chesler, *Women and Madness.*

14. Brenton, *The American Male*, p. 233.

CHAPTER 8

1. Lee Parr McGrath and Joan Scobey, *What is a Father? Children's Responses* (Essandess Special Edition, New York: Simon & Schuster, 1973).

2. Johann Jacob Bachofen, *Myth, Religion and Mother Right: Selected Writings* (New York: Bollingen Foundation Series Inc., 1967), p. 133.

3. Bronislaw Malinowski, *Sex and Repression in Savage Society*, (New York: World Publishing Co., 1970).

4. Te Rangi Hiroa (Sir Peter Buck), *The Coming of the Maori*, (Wellington: Whitcombe and Tombs, Ltd. 1966), p. 435-41.

5. Joseph Campbell, *The Masks of God: Primitive Mythology* (New York: Viking Press, 1970), pp. 351-52.

6. Elizabeth Gould Davis, *The First Sex* (Baltimore: Penguin Books, 1971); Sibylle von Cles-Reden, *The Realm of the Great Goddess*, (London: Thames and Hudson, 1961); E. O. James, *The Cult of the Mother Goddess*, (London: Thames and Hudson, 1959); Joseph Campbell, *The Masks of God*, 4 vols. (New York: Viking Press, 1970).

7. James Mellaart, *Catal Huyuk, A Neolithic Town in Anatolia* (New York: McGraw-Hill Book Co., 1967).

8. Helen Diner, *Mothers and Amazons* (Anchor Books; Garden City, N.Y.: Doubleday & Co., 1973).

9. Margaret Mead, *Male and Female* (New York: Dell Books, 1949); Mead, *Sex and Temperament in Three Primitive Societies* (Dell, 1935).

10. Michelle Zimbalist Rosaldo, "Women, Culture, and Society: A Theoretical Overview," in *Women, Culture and Society* (Stanford: Stanford University Press, 1975).

11. Colin Turnbull, *The Forest People* (New York: Simon & Schuster, 1961);

190   *Fathering: Fact or Fable?*

tB. Malinowski, *The Father and Primitive Psychology* (New York: W. W. Norton & Co., 1966).

12. Nancy Tanner, "Matrifocality in Indonesia and Africa and Among Black Americans," in *Women, Culture and Society*.

13. Margaret Mead, *Male and Female*.

14. B. Malinowski, *Father and Primitive Psychology*.

15. *Los Angeles Times*, October 6, 1974, IV, 1.

16. Harriet Holter, *Sex Roles and Social Structure*, (Oslo: Universitetsforlaget, 1970).

17. Brenton, *The American Male*; Warren Farrell, *The Liberated Man* (New York: Bantam Books, 1975).

18. Gary L. Ackerman, "Child Care Leave For Fathers?" *Ms.*, September, 1973, p. 118.

19. "Working Fathers: Views of Ten Fathers," *Ms.*, 2 (May, 1974), 55.

20. Gordon J. Hazlitt, "Notes on Notes from the 1000-Year Lifetime," *Pomona Today*, March, 1975, p. 1.

21. "Working Fathers," p. 111.

22. McGrath and Scobey, *What is a Father?*

23. Lindsy Van Gelder and Carrie Carmichael, "But What About Our Sons?" *Ms.*, 4 (October, 1975), 52.

24. *Ibid.*, p. 52.

25. Charlotte Zolotow, *William's Doll* (New York: Harper & Row, 1972).

26. "Kids Take On 'William's Doll'," *Ms.*, 2 (May, 1974).

27. Jean Baker Miller, "New Issues, New Approaches" *Psychoanalysis and Women* (Baltimore: Penguin Books, 1973) p. 396.

28. Ackerman, "Child Care Leave."

29. Rosaldo, *Women, Culture, and Society*; A. R. Radcliffe-Brown, *The Andaman Islanders* (New York: The Free Press, 1964); John Nance, *The Gentle Tasaday* (New York: Harcourt Brace Jovanovich, 1975).

31. Rosaldo, *Women, Culture, and Society*, p. 42.

32. Miller, "New Issues," pp. 395-96.

33. Eleanor Emmons Maccoby and Carol Nagy Jacklin, *The Psychology of Sex Differences* (Stanford: Stanford University Press, 1974).

34. Gerald Jonas, "Jonas and Daughters," *Ms.*, 2 (May, 1974), 57.

35. Mike Collins, "The Wright Brothers First Flew on a Kitty Hawk," *Flight Time*, Western Airlines, October, 1975, p. 15.

Stein Ed